good cooking

Exciting Entertaining

Published by:

R&R Publications Marketing Pty. Ltd

ACN 083 612 579

PO Box 254, Carlton North, Victoria 3054 Australia

Phone (61 3) 9381 2199 Fax (61 3) 9381 2689

E-mail: info@randrpublications.com.au

Web: www.randrpublications.com.au

Good Cooking Exciting Entertaining

Publisher: Richard Carroll

Creative Director: Lucy Adams

Production Manager: Anthony Carroll

Computer Graphics: Lucy Adams

Food Photography: Steve Baxter, Phillip Wilkins, David Munns, Thomas Odulate, Christine Hanscomb, Gary Smith, Warren Webb and Frank Wieder

Home Economist: Sara Buenfeld, Emma Patmore, Nancy McDougall, Louise Pickford, Jane Stevenson, Oded Schwartz, Alison Austin and Jane Lawrie

Food Stylists: Helen Payne, Sue Russell, Sam Scott, Antonia Gaunt Ellen Argyriou and Oded Schwartz

Recipe Development: Terry Farris, Jacqueline Bellefontaine, Ellen Argyriou Becky Johnson, Valerie Barrett, Emma Patmore, Geri Richards, Pam Mallender, Jan Fullwood and Tamara Milstein (www.tamaraskitchen.com) pages 12, 22, 76, 90, 140

Nutritional Consultant: Moya de Wet BSc SRD

Proof Reader: Lily Green

Includes Index

ISBN 1 74022 261 X

EAN 9 781740 222 617

First Edition Printed September 2003

Computer Typeset in Times New Roman, Verdana, Helvetica, Shelley Allegro & Humanist

Printed in Singapore by Saik Wah Press Pte Ltd

good cooking

Contents

Exciting Entertaining

Do you enjoy entertaining and look forward to welcoming family and friends into your home? Or do you find it a chore and avoid having people over? Let's face it – at some stage, we all wonder what we can make for friends and family that is simple to prepare yet stylish, looks delightful, and tastes good! Now, you don't need to wonder. Discover how easy, enjoyable, and exciting entertaining can be with Exciting Entertaining. The recipes in this book will make you want to cook for your friends and family!

Exciting Entertaining offers you a wide range of recipe choices for your occasion. There is something for everyone. Whether you're planning a simple dinner for four, a romantic dinner for two, a special occasion for all the family, or a fun and casual gathering for friends – you will find dishes to suit all tastes, budgets, and events. There are some old favorites, plus new and exciting recipes featuring oriental or Mediterranean ingredients that you will find in specialty supermarkets or delicatessens. All recipes use the freshest and best ingredients and are inspired by today's busy lifestyle. And each recipe is enhanced by a stunning photograph that suggest ways to serve the dish and the accompaniments to offer.

Exciting Entertaining is divided into clearly marked sections for easy use. There are recipes for seafood, poultry, pork, meat, barbecue, vegetables, and desserts. Within most sections you will also find recipes for appetizers, starters, and mains, to help you with planning menus for your special events. All recipes have easy-to-follow instructions, and most have a note providing you with an interesting fact or suggestion to extend the recipe and your knowledge of food and cooking.

Take your entertaining to a new level with Exciting Entertaining. This book will help you experience success every time you entertain. The recipes will satisfy and impress your guests and, above all, encourage you to enjoy entertaining and approach any special occasion with confidence. Allow this book to become an important part of your cooking library and of entertaining for you and your family and friends.

Seafood can be prepared in many ways: marinated, steamed, stir-fried, baked, and smoked. Seafood goes well with cilantro, chili, butter, dill, lemon grass, parsley, pine nuts and lemon.

Seafood

Seafood Soups

Hot and Sour Shrimp Soup

Ingredients

2¼ lb/1 kg medium uncooked shrimps

1 tbsp vegetable oil

8 slices fresh or bottled galangal
   or fresh ginger

8 kaffir lime leaves

2 stalks fresh lemon grass, bruised,
   or 1 tsp dried lemon grass,
   soaked in hot water until soft

2 fresh red chilies, halved and seeded

8 cups water

3 tbsp fresh cilantro leaves

1 fresh red chili, chopped

2 tbsp lime juice

2 kaffir lime leaves, shredded

Method

1 Shell and devein the shrimps, and set aside. Reserve the heads and shells. Heat the oil in a large saucepan over a high heat, add the shrimp heads and shells and cook, stirring, for 5 minutes or until the shells change color. Stir in the galangal or fresh ginger, lime leaves, lemon grass, halved chilies, and water, cover and bring to simmering point. Simmer, stirring occasionally, for 15 minutes.

2 Strain the liquid into a clean saucepan and discard the solids. Add the shrimps and cook for 2 minutes. Stir in the cilantro, chopped chili and lime juice, and cook for 1 minute or until the shrimps are tender.

3 Ladle the soup into bowls and garnish with the shredded lime leaves.

Serves 4

Shrimp and Chicken Soup

Ingredients

1 tbsp vegetable oil

1 onion, diced

1 red bell pepper, diced

2 cloves garlic, crushed

1 tsp finely chopped fresh ginger

4 cups chicken bouillon

4¹/₂ oz/125 g boneless chicken thigh or breast fillets, sliced

20 uncooked small shrimps, shelled and deveined

4¹/₂ oz/125 g rice noodles

4¹/₂ oz/125 g canned bamboo shoots, drained and sliced

5 white mushrooms, thinly sliced

¹/₄ lettuce, shredded

2 scallions, thinly sliced

2 tbsp finely chopped fresh cilantro

1¹/₂ tbsp soy sauce

freshly ground black pepper

Method

1 Heat the oil in a saucepan over a medium heat, add the onion and red bell pepper and cook, stirring, for 5 minutes or until the onion is soft. Add the garlic and ginger and cook for 2 minutes longer.

2 Stir in the bouillon and bring to the boil. Add the chicken, shrimp, noodles, bamboo shoots, and mushrooms, reduce heat and simmer for 5 minutes or until the noodles are tender.

3 Stir in the lettuce, scallions, cilantro, soy sauce, and black pepper to taste and serve immediately.

Serves 4

Spanish Fish Soup with Saffron

Ingredients

2 tbsp olive oil

2 large carrots, finely chopped

3 leeks, finely sliced and well washed

1 red bell pepper, chopped

1 green bell pepper, chopped

1 tbsp Spanish paprika

large pinch saffron threads

2 cups white wine

3 cups fish bouillon

14 oz/400 g firm white fish fillets, diced

14 oz/400 g shrimps, shelled and deveined

14 oz/400 g baby calamari or squid

2 tbsp chopped parsley

1 lemon, cut into 6 wedges

Method

1 Heat the olive oil in a large saucepan, add the carrots, leeks, and bell peppers and sauté until softened about 10 minutes. Add the paprika and saffron, continuing to cook for a few more minutes.

2 Add the wine and bouillon, and bring the soup to the boil, simmering for 15 minutes.

3 Add the diced fish, shelled shrimp, and squid and simmer for a further 5 minutes. Sprinkle the with parsley, and serve with a wedge of lemon.

Serves 6

Clam Chowder

Ingredients

9 oz/255 g butter

6 bacon strips, finely chopped

3 onions, finely chopped

1 stalk celery, finely chopped

1 cup all-purpose flour

5 cups milk

3 cups fish bouillon

5 potatoes, boiled and finely diced

2¼ lb/1 kg clam meat

salt and pepper

snipped chives

cream

whole clams, steamed open
  for garnish

Method

1 Melt the butter in a saucepan, and add the bacon, onion, and celery. Cook for 5 minutes or until tender. Add the flour and cook, stirring, for 2 minutes.

2 Add the milk, fish bouillon, and potatoes, and cover and simmer for 10 minutes. Add the clam meat and cook more for 10 minutes. Season to taste.

3 Serve, scattered with the snipped chives, in a deep plate with the cream, parsley and clams in the shell.

Serves 8–10

Thai Shrimp Soup with Lemon Grass

Ingredients

10¹/₂ oz/300 g large green shrimp

3 stalks lemon grass

4 cups fish bouillon

³/₄ in/2 cm piece ginger, peeled and
    cut into fine strips

2 kaffir lime leaves

¹/₂ small pineapple, peeled and cored

1 tbsp fish sauce

1 tbsp lime juice

6 scallions, thinly sliced on
    the diagonal

fresh cilantro leaves

pepper to taste

6 lime wedges to serve

Method

1 Peel and devein the shrimps, leaving the tails intact. Reserve the shells and discard the veins. Halve the lemon grass stalks and squash the bases with the flat side of a knife.

2 Place the shrimp shells in a medium saucepan with the bouillon and bring slowly to the boil. Reduce the heat and simmer gently for 10 minutes. Strain, return to the saucepan and add the lemon grass, ginger, and lime leaves and return to simmering point.

3 Cut the pineapple into thin pieces and add to the bouillon along with the shrimps. Simmer just until the shrimps turn pink and tender (a few minutes, depending on their size). Add the fish sauce, lime juice, scallions, and cilantro.

4 Remove the lemon grass and lime leaves, season with pepper and serve immediately with a wedge of lime.

Serves 6

Rustic Mediterranean Seafood Soup

Ingredients

7 oz/200 g calamari tubes, cleaned

10 oz/285 g green shrimps

7 oz/200 g mussels

9 oz/255 g mixed firm white fish fillets
   (red mullet, sea perch, red fish)

1 tbsp olive oil

2 cloves garlic, crushed

1 onion, finely chopped

1/2 cup white wine

14 oz/400 g canned diced tomatoes

4 cups fish bouillon

pinch saffron

2 potatoes, peeled and cut into
   large cubes

crusty Italian bread to serve

Method

1 Cut the calamari tubes into rings. Peel and devein the shrimps, leaving the tails intact. Scrub the mussels and debeard, discarding any that are already open. Remove any bones from the fish and cut into large pieces.

2 Heat the oil in a large saucepan. Add the garlic and onion and cook over a medium heat for 3 minutes or until the onion is golden. Add the white wine and bring to the boil. Cook over a high heat until nearly all the liquid has been absorbed.

3 Add the tomatoes, fish bouillon, saffron, and potatoes and simmer for 15 minutes or until the potatoes are tender. Do not overcook or the potatoes will start to break up.

4 Add all the seafood and simmer for 3–5 minutes or until tender. Serve with crusty Italian bread.

Serves 6

Seafood Starters

Italian Tuna and Bean Salad

Ingredients

7 oz/200 g can tuna in oil, drained and oil reserved

14 oz/400g can borlotti beans, drained and rinsed

1 small red onion, thinly sliced

2 stalks celery, thinly sliced

3 tbsp chopped fresh Italian parsley

Dressing:

4 tbsp olive oil

2 tbsp balsamic or white wine vinegar

salt and black pepper

Method

1 To make the dressing, whisk the reserved tuna oil with the olive oil and vinegar, then season.

2 Flake the tuna into a large bowl and mix with the borlotti beans, red onion, celery, and parsley. Spoon over the dressing and toss well to combine.

Note: The combination of colors, flavors and textures in this simple salad has made it a real favourite in Italy. It's delicious served with some warmed ciabatta bread.

Serves 4

San Franciscan Seafood Chowder in Bread Cups

Ingredients

8 smallish round loaves of bread

3 oz/85 g butter

2 leeks, well washed and finely sliced

2 onions, finely chopped

4 cloves garlic, minced

2 carrots, peeled and chopped

1 parsnip, peeled and chopped

2 stalks celery, finely sliced

1 tbsp fresh thyme leaves

$^1\!/_2$ cup all-purpose flour

8 cups fish bouillon

2$^1\!/_4$ lb/1 kg mixed seafood, including shrimps, mussels, clams, squid, and white fish

7 fl oz/200 mL thick cream

$^1\!/_2$ bunch parsley, chopped

salt and pepper to taste

juice of 1 large lemon

$^1\!/_2$ bunch chives, chopped

Method

1 Preheat the oven to 400°F/200°C/Gas Mark 6. First, prepare the bread cups. Using a sharp knife, cut a large hole in the top of each bread loaf, then remove the crusty top and set aside. Carefully remove all the soft bread from inside of loaves, leaving the surrounding crust intact.

2 Place the loaves in the preheated oven and bake for 15 minutes until crisp and dry. Set aside.

3 Melt the butter in a large saucepan, and add the chopped leeks, onions, garlic, carrots, parsnip, celery, and thyme leaves. Sauté in the butter for 10 minutes until vegetables are soft and golden. Remove the sauce pan from the heat, and sprinkle the flour over the vegetables, stirring constantly to mix the flour with the butter. Return to the heat and continue stirring until the mixture begins to turn golden (about 2 minutes). This gives flour a 'cooked' flavor.

4 Add the fish bouillon, stirring constantly to dissolve the roux mixture into the liquid, then simmer the chowder for 20 minutes. Meanwhile, prepare the seafood by cutting the fish and shellfish into bite-sized pieces.

5 Add all the seafood, cream, parsley and salt and pepper (to taste) to the chowder, and cook for 5 minutes. Do not allow the chowder to boil rapidly because it may curdle. Once the shellfish has cooked, stir the lemon juice through the chowder. Then, ladle the chowder into the bread cups. Garnish with the chopped chives and serve.

Serves 8

Shrimp and Avocado Cocktail

Ingredients

14 oz/400 g cooked peeled shrimps, defrosted if frozen

8 tbsp mayonnaise

4 tbsp tomato ketchup

2 stalks celery, finely chopped

1 scallion, finely sliced, or 1 tbsp finely chopped onion

salt and black pepper

2 avocados

squeeze of lemon juice

Method

1 Mix together the shrimps, mayonnaise, and tomato ketchup in a bowl, then stir in the celery, scallion or onion and season to taste.

2 Halve the avocados, remove the stones, and peel. Dice the flesh, then toss in the lemon juice to stop it browning. Add to the shrimp mixture, stirring lightly, then transfer to glasses or serving plates, and grind over a little pepper.

Note: This is a classic starter that's even better when you add chunks of ripe avocado. This gives four generous portions, so you could also serve it with crisp leaves as a salad.

Serves 4

Sardines Stuffed with Spinach and Pine Nuts

Ingredients

8 fresh sardines

2 tbsp olive oil

1 shallot, finely chopped

1 tbsp pine nut kernels

6 oz/175 g frozen leaf spinach, defrosted and excess moisture squeezed out

1 tbsp golden raisins

2 tbsp fresh breadcrumbs

1 tbsp lime juice

Method

1 Preheat the oven to 425°F/220°C/Gas Mark 7. Remove the scales from the fish by scraping from the tail end with the back of a small knife. Cut off the heads, then slice along the belly and remove the guts. Open out each fish and place skin-side up on the work surface. Press along the length of the backbone with your thumb, then turn the fish over and ease out the backbone, cutting it at the tail end but leaving the tail intact. Rinse and pat dry with kitchen towels, season and turn in 1 tablespoon of the oil.

2 Heat the remaining oil in a frying pan, and fry the shallot and pine nut kernels for 2–3 minutes, until golden. Remove from the heat, then stir in the spinach, golden raisins, 1 tablespoon of the breadcrumbs, and lime juice. Season, then use the mixture to sandwich the sardines together in pairs, skin-side out.

3 Lay the sardines on a baking sheet, sprinkle with the remaining breadcrumbs, and bake for 10 minutes or until golden and cooked through.

Note: Fresh sardines are easy to fillet, and this fruit, nut, and spinach filling will change your view of them for ever!

Serves 4

Red Mullet Saltimbocca

Ingredients

**4 red mullet, about 9 oz/255 g
  each, filleted**

salt and black pepper

16 fresh sage leaves

**4 thin slices prosciutto crudo,
  halved lengthways**

1 oz/30 g butter

2 tbsp olive oil

lemon wedges to serve

Method

1 Wipe the fish fillets, then remove any scales by scraping from the tail end with the back of a knife. Remove any fine bones with a pair of tweezers.

2 Season lightly, then press 2 sage leaves onto 1 side of each fillet, and wrap in a slice of prosciutto. Cover and leave in the refrigerator for 30 minutes, or up to 8 hours to allow the flavors to mingle.

3 Heat the butter and oil in a large frying pan. Place the fish in the pan, sage-side down, and cook for 2–3 minutes, until crisp. Turn over and cook for a further 2–3 minutes, until the fish is opaque and the outside crisp and deep red. Serve with lemon wedges.

Note: Red mullet tastes delicious in this crispy prosciutto wrapping, which helps to stop the fish drying out as it cooks. But make sure you remove all the small bones from the fish.

Serves 4

Spicy Deep-Fried Squid Rings

Ingredients

6 tbsp all-purpose flour

2 tbsp paprika

1 tsp salt

1 lb/455 g fresh squid, cut into rings, or frozen squid rings, defrosted and dried

vegetable oil for deep-frying

Method

1 Mix together the flour, paprika and salt. Toss the squid rings in the seasoned flour to coat evenly.

2 Heat 2 in/5 cm of vegetable oil in a large heavy-based saucepan. Test that the oil is ready by adding a squid ring – it should sizzle at once. Cook $\frac{1}{4}$ of the rings for 1-2 minutes, until golden. Drain on kitchen towels and keep warm while you cook the remaining rings in 3 more batches.

Note: Deep-fried squid rings are always good when they're freshly made – these have a little extra spice. Serve them as a starter or a pre-dinner nibble with a little mayonnaise.

Serves 4

Thai Fish Sticks with Cucumber Salad

Ingredients

4 scallions, chopped

small handful of fresh cilantro

1 lb/455 g cod loin or other skinless white fish fillet, cubed

3 tbsp red curry paste

1 tsp salt

2 tsp lime juice

1 large egg white

12 stalks lemon grass

Salad

1/2 cucumber, peeled and very thinly sliced

4 tbsp white wine vinegar

4 tbsp superfine sugar

1 large red or green chili, deseeded and finely chopped

1 small shallot, thinly sliced

Method

1 To make the salad, combine the cucumber, vinegar, sugar, chili and shallot with 4 tablespoons of cold water. Cover and leave in a cool place until needed.

2 To make the fish sticks, blend the scallions and cilantro in a food processor until finely chopped, or use a hand blender. Add the fish, curry paste, salt, and lime juice, and blend until the fish is finely chopped. Add the egg white and continue blending until the mixture is stiff.

3 Divide the fish mixture into 12 portions, then carefully press each around a lemon grass stick, forming a 'sausage' shape. Preheat the broiler to high. Place the fish sticks on a lightly oiled baking sheet, then broil for 6 minutes, turning once, until cooked and lightly browned on all sides. Serve with the cucumber salad.

Note: Cooking these spicy kebabs on lemon grass sticks gives them a lovely citrus flavor. The simple salad combines slivers of cool cucumber with a little red-hot chili.

Serves 4

Seafood Mains

Lobster Provencale

Ingredients

2 oz/55 g butter

1 tsp freshly crushed garlic

2 scallions, chopped

11 oz/310 g can tomatoes

**salt and cracked black peppercorns
  to taste**

pinch saffron

1 large lobster, cooked

¹/₄ cup brandy

boiled rice

¹/₂ bunch fresh chives, chopped

lemon wedges to serve

Method

1 In a shallow frying pan melt the butter over a moderate heat. Add the garlic, scallions, tomatoes, salt and pepper, and saffron. Cook until the onions are translucent (about 2 minutes).

2 Remove the meat from the lobster, and cut into large pieces. Add the lobster to the frying pan, and flame with the brandy. Cook gently until the lobster is heated through.

3 Place the rice on a serving plate, and sprinkle with the chives.

4 Remove the lobster from the frying pan, retaining the cooking liquid as a sauce. Arrange the lobster on the rice, and spoon the sauce over the lobster.
Serve with lemon wedges.

Serves 4

Lemon-Scented Fish Pie

Ingredients

**2¹/₄ lb/1 kg potatoes, cut into
even-sized pieces**

2 oz/55 g butter

1 onion, chopped

2 stalks celery, sliced

2 tbsp all-purpose flour

1 cup fish bouillon

**finely grated rind and juice of
1 large lemon**

salt and black pepper

**1 lb/455 g cod or other white fish,
cut into cubes**

6 oz/170 g mussels, cooked and shelled

2 tbsp chopped fresh parsley

4 tbsp milk

Method

1 Cook the potatoes in boiling salted water for 15–20 minutes or until tender, then drain.

2 Meanwhile, melt 1 oz/30 g of the butter in a large saucepan, then add the onion and celery, and cook for 2–3 minutes or until softened. Add the flour and cook, stirring, for 1 minute, then slowly add the fish bouillon and cook, stirring, until thickened. Add the lemon rind and juice and season with pepper.

3 Preheat the oven to 425°F/220°C/Gas Mark 7. Remove the sauce from the heat, stir in the cod, mussels, and parsley, then transfer to an ovenproof dish. Mash the potatoes with the remaining butter and the milk. Season, then spread evenly over the fish with a fork. Cook in the oven for 30–40 minutes, until the sauce is bubbling and the topping is starting to brown.

Serves 4

Grilled Lobster with Chili Salsa

Ingredients

2 cooked lobsters, about
   12 oz/ 340 g each
4 tsp olive oil
cayenne pepper

Salsa
2 tbsp olive oil
1 red bell pepper, deseeded and diced
1 small onion, chopped
1 large red chili, deseeded and
   finely chopped
1 tbsp sun-dried tomato paste
salt and black pepper

Method

1 To make the Salsa, heat the oil in a saucepan and fry the red bell pepper, onion, and chili for 5 minutes or until tender. Stir in the tomato paste and season to taste. Transfer to a bowl.

2 To cut the lobsters in half lengthways, turn 1 on its back. Cut through the head end first, using a large, sharp knife, then turn the lobster around and cut through the tail end. Discard the small greyish 'sac' in the head; everything else in the shell is edible. Crack the large claws with a small hammer or wooden rolling pin. Repeat with the second lobster. Drizzle the cut side of the lobsters with the oil and sprinkle with the cayenne pepper.

3 Heat a large non-stick frying pan or ridged cast-iron grill pan until very hot, then add the lobster halves, cut-side down, and cook for 2–3 minutes, until lightly golden. Serve with the salsa.

Serves 2

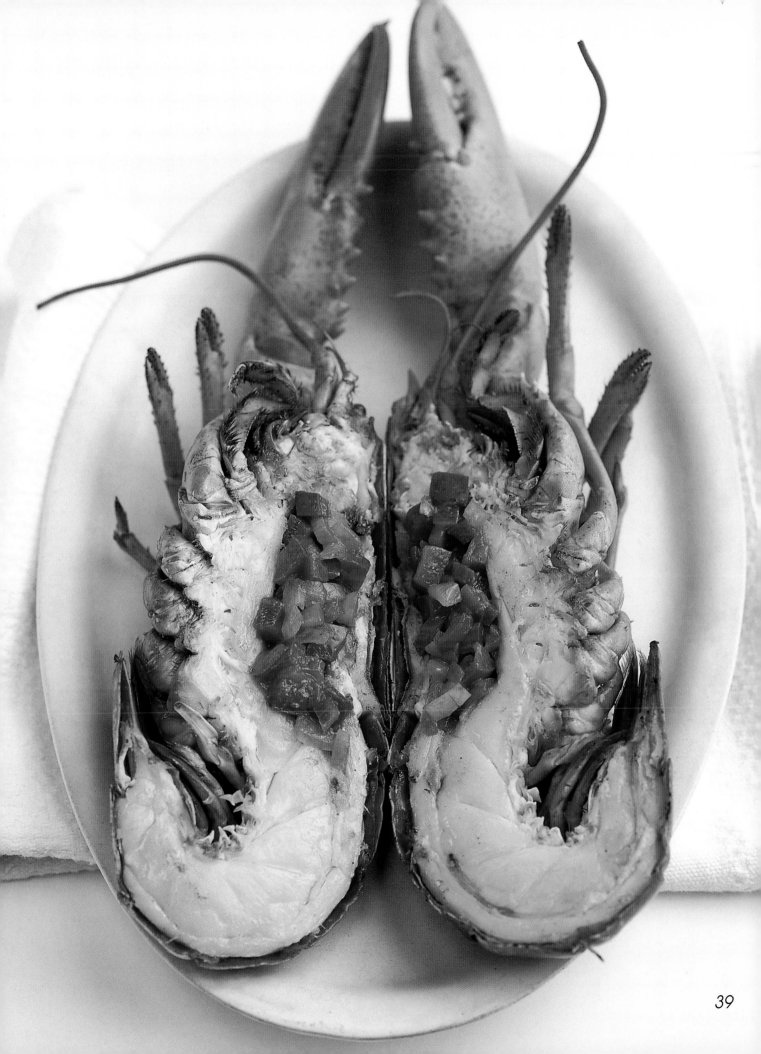

Spaghettini and Scallops with Breadcrumbs

Ingredients

12 fresh scallops with their corals

1/2 cup extra virgin olive oil

1/4 cup dried white breadcrumbs

4 tbsp chopped fresh Italian parsley

2 cloves garlic, finely chopped

1 tsp crushed dried chilies

12 oz/340 g dried spaghettini

salt

4 tbsp dry white wine

Method

1 Detach the corals from the scallops and set aside. Slice each white part into 3 or 4 pieces. Heat 2 tablespoons of the oil in a frying pan, then add the breadcrumbs and fry, stirring, for 3 minutes or until golden. Remove from the frying pan and set aside.

2 Heat 5 tablespoons of the oil in the frying pan, then add 2 tablespoons of the parsley, the garlic and chilies, and fry for 2 minutes or until their flavors are released. Meanwhile, cook the spaghettini in plenty of boiling salted water, until tender but still firm to the bite. Drain, return to the saucepan and toss with the remaining oil.

3 Stir the white parts of the scallops into the frying pan and fry for 30 seconds or until starting to turn opaque. Add the wine and the reserved scallop corals, cook for 30 seconds, then add the spaghettini and cook for 1 minute, tossing to combine. Sprinkle with the breadcrumbs and remaining parsley.

Serves 4

Bouillabaisse

Ingredients

6³/₄ lb/3 kg mixed fish and seafood,
   including firm white fish fillets, shrimps,
   mussels, crab, and calamari rings

¹/₄ cup olive oil

2 cloves garlic, crushed

2 large onions, chopped

2 leeks, sliced

2 x 14 oz/400 g cans tomatoes, drained
   and mashed

1 tbsp chopped fresh thyme or
   1 tsp dried thyme

2 tbsp chopped fresh basil or
   1 ¹/₂ tsp dried basil

2 tbsp chopped fresh parsley

2 bay leaves

2 tbsp finely grated orange rind

1 tsp saffron threads

1 cup dry white wine

1 cup fish bouillon

freshly ground black pepper

Method

1 Remove the bones and skin from the fish fillets and cut into ³/₄ in/2 cm cubes. Peel and devein the shrimps, leaving the tails intact. Scrub and remove the beards from the mussels. Cut the crab into quarters. Set aside.

2 Heat the oil in a large saucepan over a medium heat, add the garlic, onions, and leeks, and cook for 5 minutes or until the onions are golden. Add the tomatoes, thyme, basil, parsley, bay leaves, orange rind, saffron, wine, and bouillon, and bring to the boil. Reduce the heat and simmer for 30 minutes.

3 Add the fish and crab and cook for 10 minutes. Add the remaining seafood and cook for 5 minutes or until the fish and seafood are cooked. Season to taste with freshly ground black pepper.

Serves 6

Mussels Tin Tin

Ingredients

1/2 cup white wine

1 red chili, sliced

1 stalk lemon grass, crushed

1 tbsp fresh chopped ginger

1 clove garlic, chopped

2 1/4 lb/1 kg mussels, cleaned and
  beards removed

1 tbsp peanut oil

1/3 cup coconut cream

1 tbsp fresh cilantro, chopped

Method

1 Put the white wine, chili, lemon grass, ginger, and garlic in a pot and infuse together for 15 minutes.

2 Put the mussels in a casserole with the oil, and add the infusion.

3 Add the coconut cream and cook until the mussels have opened, stirring frequently. Discard any mussels that do not open. Stir in the cilantro and serve.

Serves 4

Grilled Salmon Fillets

Ingredients

4 x Atlantic salmon fillets

I cup dry red wine

¹/₂ cup olive oil

¹/₂ cup lemon juice

2 shallots, chopped

2 tsp freshly crushed garlic

I tsp freshly chopped ginger

I tsp salt

¹/₂ tsp rosemary leaves

¹/₄ tsp tabasco

4 large bell pepper rings

4 large slices white onion

Method

1 Rinse the salmon under cold running water, pat dry, and set aside.

2 In a shallow glass bowl, combine all but the last 2 ingredients. Place the salmon in the marinade. Cover and refrigerate for 1–2 hours.

3 Remove from the refrigerator and bring to room temperature. Remove the salmon from the marinade and reserve the liquid.

4 Cook the salmon, bell pepper, and onion on a well-oiled barbecue or broiler over medium heat for 6–7 minutes or until lightly browned.

5 Baste with the marinade, turn, and baste again. Continue cooking for another 5 minutes or until the flesh is opaque when fork-tested.

6 To serve, top the fillets with the bell pepper and onions.

Serves 4

Abalone Chowder

Ingredients

2 strips bacon, cut into 1 in/2½ cm-pieces

1 medium onion, chopped

3 tsp freshly crushed garlic

2 stalks celery, chopped

1 large carrot, chopped

½ tsp freshly chopped chili

16 oz/455 g can tomato pieces

2 tbsp tomato paste

2 bay leaves

1 heaped tsp thyme leaves

½ tsp salt

½ tsp black peppercorns, freshly ground

1 cup fish bouillon

6 cups water

1 lb/455 g abalone steaks, ground or finely chopped

2 medium pontiac potatoes, diced

2 tbsp all-purpose flour

2 tbsp water

2 ice cubes

½ cup dry sherry

Method

1 Fry the bacon in a large frying pan until crisp. Pour off almost all the fat, keeping a small amount. Fry the onion, garlic, celery, carrot, and chili in the remaining bacon fat.

2 Cook for 3–4 minutes until the vegetables are tender. Add the tomatoes, including the juice, tomato paste, bay leaves, thyme, and salt and pepper. Stir in the fish bouillon, water, abalone, and potatoes. Bring the mixture to the boil, then reduce the heat to simmer. Simmer, uncovered, for 40–45 minutes.

3 In a jar with a tight-fitting lid, combine the flour, water and ice cubes. Shake the jar vigorously, then pour the flour and water paste into the chowder. Add the sherry. Stir and increase the heat until the liquid boils. Allow the mixture to boil gently until the broth thickens slightly.

4 Taste for seasoning, and add more sherry and salt and pepper if desired.

Serves 10

Spanish-Style Fish Chops

Ingredients

4 jewfish chops

olive oil

1 tbsp parsley flakes

3 tsp freshly crushed garlic

1½ tbsp almonds, slivered

1 tbsp shallots, chopped

½ tsp ground paprika

½ tsp lemon rind, grated

425 g/15 oz can tomatoes, drained and roughly chopped

Method

1 Preheat the oven a to moderate temperature 350°F/180°C/Gas Mark 4.

2 Arrange the fish in a shallow ovenproof dish that has been lightly brushed with the olive oil. Brush the top of each cutlet with the olive oil.

3 Combine the parsley, garlic, almonds, shallots, paprika, lemon rind and, 1½ tablespoons of the olive oil. Spoon over the fish, and press down well.

4 Bake the fish in a the preheated oven for 10 minutes.

5 Pour the tomatoes around the fish, and cook for a further 10 minutes or until fish is cooked.

Serves 4

51

Chili Crab

Ingredients

2 x 1²/₃ lb/750 g mud crabs, cooked

3 tsp freshly chopped chili

1 small red chili, chopped

2 tsp freshly chopped ginger

3 tsp freshly crushed garlic

¹/₂ cup vegetable oil

1¹/₄ cup chunky-style tomato sauce

2 tbsp brown sugar

²/₃ cup boiling water

salt

1 egg, beaten

fresh cilantro leaves for garnish

Accompaniments

1 cucumber, cut into chunks

crisp French bread, cut into thick slices

Method

1 Remove the large claws from each crab and crack at the joints. Use a hammer (or rolling pin) and crack the broadest part of the shell cleanly taking care not to splinter the shell. Turn each crab on its back with its tail-flap towards you. Tap around the fault line with a hammer and push the body out of each shell. Discard the stomach sac and the lungs.

2 Leave the creamy brown meat in the shell, and break in half. Cut the lower half of the body in half and crack the smaller claws.

3 Pound the fresh chilies, ginger, and garlic to a fine paste with a mortar and pestle or chop up in a food processor.

4 Heat the oil in a hot wok or a heavy-bottomed saucepan, add the paste, and cook gently without browning or until the mixture gives off a spicy aroma.

5 Add the tomato sauce, brown sugar, boiling water and salt to taste.

6 When the sauce is bubbling, toss in the crabs, and mix to ensure the crabs are coated in the sauce. Add the beaten egg, which will become almost scrambled in the sauce.

7 Spoon onto a warmed serving bowl, and sprinkle with the cilantro leaves. Serve immediately, with the cucumber and bread accompaniments.

Serves 4

53

Sesame Barbecued Shrimps

Ingredients

2¼ lb/1 kg medium-large king shrimps

¼ cup olive oil

¼ cup red wine

4 shallots, finely chopped

1 tsp grated lemon rind

½ tsp cracked black peppercorns

**12 bamboo skewers, soaked in water
   for 30 minutes**

½ cup toasted sesame seeds

Method

1 Peel and devein the shrimps, leaving the shell tails intact.

2 Combine the oil, wine, shallots, lemon rind and pepper. Mix well.

3 Thread the shrimps onto the bamboo skewers, approximately 3 per skewer.

4 Place the skewers in a shallow dish and pour the marinade over. Allow to marinate for at least 1 hour.

5 Roll the shrimps in the toasted sesame seeds, pressing them on well. Refrigerate for 30 minutes before cooking. Brush with the marinade during cooking. Serve immediately.

Serves 6-8

Fish in a Parcel

Ingredients

4 mackerel chops

freshly ground black peppercorns

1 tbsp lemon juice

¼ tsp tasty cheese, grated

4 scallions, chopped

1 medium cucumber, sliced

Method

1 Preheat the oven to a moderate temperature 350°F/180°C/Gas Mark 4.

2 Place each chop on a piece of greased, heavy-duty foil. Season with the pepper and lemon juice.

3 Divide the grated cheese among the chops. Sprinkle with scallions, and top each chop with the cucumber slices (about 4–6 slices on each chop).

4 Wrap the foil around the chop and seal. Place on an oven tray and bake in the preheated, oven for 20–25 minutes.

Serves 4

Chinese Garfish Fillets Mesclun and Sweet Chili Sauce

Ingredients

2 oz/55 g Szechwan pepper, crushed

1 cup corn starch

1¹/₂ tsp Chinese five spice powder

2 oz/55 g salt

2¹/₄ lb/1 kg garfish fillets, all bones removed, skin on

mesclun to serve

Sweet Chili Sauce

3 large red chilies

4 tsp freshly crushed garlic

4 cilantro roots

1 cup sugar

¹/₂ cup Thai coconut vinegar

¹/₂ cup water

3 tbsp cilantro leaves

2 tbsp Thai fish sauce

Method

1 Blend the Szechwan pepper, corn starch, five spice powder, and salt together, and sieve. Lightly coat the garfish fillets, then deep-fry at 350°F/180°C for 1–2 minutes.

2 To make the Sweet Chili Sauce, chop the chilis, garlic and cilantro roots finely. Boil the sugar, Thai vinegar, and water together. Remove from the heat and add the chilis and cilantro roots, garlic, cilantro leaves, and fish sauce.

3 To serve, place the mesclun salad and fish on a serving plate with the Sweet Chili Sauce as a dipping sauce in a small dish on the side.

Note: The Sweet Chili Sauce will have a long life if kept in refrigerator.

Serves 6

Lobster Newburg

Ingredients

2 oz/55 g butter

4¹/₂ lb/2 kg lobster, boiled, shelled, and cut into small pieces

2 tsp salt

¹/₄ tsp ground cayenne pepper

¹/₄ tsp ground nutmeg

1 cup heavy cream

4 egg yolks

2 tbsp brandy

2 tbsp dry sherry

reserved lobster-tail shell or 4–6 patty shells and rice and steamed asparagus to serve

Method

1 In a shallow frying pan, melt the butter over a moderate heat. When the foam subsides, add the lobster. Cook slowly for about 5 minutes. Add the salt, cayenne pepper, and nutmeg.

2 In a small bowl, lightly beat the cream with the egg yolks. Add the mixture to the pan, stirring continuously.

3 Finally, add the brandy and sherry as the mass begins to thicken. Do not allow to boil because the sauce will curdle.

4 Serve either: placed back in the lobster tail shell; or in patty shells. Serve with the steamed rice, and some lightly steamed asparagus.

Serves 4-6

Octopus with Potatoes and Peas

Ingredients

**2¼lb/1 kg octopus, cleaned and
  skinned**

salt

½ cup olive oil

1 large onion, chopped

4 garlic cloves, chopped

14 oz/400 g can tomatoes

¼ tsp ground chilies

**1 lb/455 g potatoes, peeled and cut
  into thick slices**

9 oz/255 g cooked peas

Method

1 Put the octopus in a large saucepan without adding water. Sprinkle with the salt, cover, and allow to cook in its own juices over a low heat for about 45 minutes.

2 Four times during the cooking, lift the octopus out, using a fork and dip into a pan of boiling water, then run the octopus under cold water and return it to the saucepan to continue cooking.

3 Heat the olive oil in an ovenproof casserole dish and gently fry the onion, garlic, tomatoes, and chili for about 10 minutes or until the onion has turned opaque. Add the potatoes and cook for about 5 minutes. Add the octopus and enough of its cooking liquid to cover the contents of the casserole. Add salt to taste, and let the dish cook gently, uncovered for about 30 minutes or until the potatoes are tender and the sauce is largely reduced.

4 Finally, add the cooked peas to the casserole and heat through. Serve the octopus and vegetables straight from the casserole.

Serves 4

Sautéed Calamari

Ingredients

3 tbsp olive oil

I large onion, sliced

2 tsp freshly crushed garlic

I tbsp sweet basil leaves

I tbsp Madras mild curry

salt and freshly ground black peppercorns

2 tbsp honey

I lb/455 g calamari rings

I tbsp parsley flakes

Method

1 Heat the oil on the barbecue plate, add the onion and garlic, and sauté until tender.

2 Stir in the basil, curry paste, salt, pepper and honey. Mix well.

3 Add the calamari rings, and gently stir the calamari a few minutes until cooked through. Stir in the parsley and serve immediately.

Serves 4

Baked Fish

Ingredients

3 ⅓ lb/1 ½ kg whole snapper

salt and pepper

juice of 1 lemon

½ cup olive oil

1 large onion, sliced

3 cloves garlic, thinly sliced

½ cup celery, chopped

15 oz/425 g can tomato
  pieces, peeled

½ cup dry white wine, optional

½ tsp sugar

1 tsp oregano

lemon or lime wedges to serve

Method

1 Prepare the fish, leaving the head and tail on. Make diagonal cuts on surface, sprinkle with a little salt and pepper and lemon juice. Set aside for 20 minutes.

2 Heat half the oil in a frying pan, and sauté the onion, garlic, and celery for 3 minutes. Add the tomatoes, the wine if using, sugar, and oregano, and season with salt and pepper. Sauté a further 2 minutes.

3 Spread the mixture into an oiled baking dish and place the fish on top. Drizzle the remaining oil over the fish. Bake in a preheated oven 350°F/180°C/Gas Mark 4 for 30–40 minutes, depending on size. Baste the fish during cooking.

4 Remove the fish to a serving platter, spoon the sauce around fish, and serve with lemon or lime wedges.

Note: This dish can be accompanied by either vegetables or salad.

Serves 4

Seafood Salads

Thai Squid Salad

Ingredients

3 squid tubes, cleaned

7 oz/200 g green beans, sliced lengthwise

2 tomatoes, cut into wedges

1 small green pawpaw, peeled, seeded and shredded

4 scallions, sliced

1½ tbsp fresh mint leaves

1½ tbsp fresh cilantro leaves

1 fresh red chili, chopped

Lime Dressing

2 tsp brown sugar

3 tbsp lime juice

1 tbsp Thai fish sauce

Method

1 Using a sharp knife, make a single cut down the length of each squid tube and open out. Cut parallel lines down the length of the squid, taking care not to cut through the flesh. Make more cuts in the opposite direction to form a diamond pattern.

2 Heat a nonstick chargrill or frying pan over a high heat, add the squid, and cook for 1–2 minutes each side or until tender. Remove from the pan and cut into thin strips.

3 Place the squid, beans, tomatoes, pawpaw, scallions, mint, cilantro, and chili in a serving bowl.

4 To make the lime dressing, place the sugar, lime juice, and fish sauce in a screwtop jar and shake well. Drizzle over the salad and toss to combine. Cover and stand for 20 minutes before serving.

Note: Serve this salad with soy rice noodles. Boil 13 oz/370 g fresh rice noodles, drain, and sprinkle with a little reduced-salt soy sauce. Scatter with toasted sesame seeds and toss to combine with the salad.

Serves 4

Warm Barbecued Octopus and Potato Salad

Ingredients

1 lb/455 g baby octopus, cleaned

1 lb/455 g pink-skinned potatoes, desiree, pontiac or pink fir, washed

arugula or mixed salad greens

2 Lebanese cucumbers, chopped

2 green onions, finely sliced

crusty bread to serve

Lime and Chili Marinade

2 tbsp olive oil

juice of 1 lime or lemon

1 fresh red chili, diced

1 clove garlic, crushed

Tomato Concasse, optional

4 plum tomatoes, diced

1/2 cup chopped fresh cilantro

1/2 red onion, diced

1/3 cup balsamic or sherry vinegar

1 tbsp olive oil

1 tbsp lemon juice

freshly ground black pepper

Method

1 To make the marinade, place the oil, lime juice, chili and garlic in a bowl. Mix to combine. Cut the octopus in half lengthwise; if very small, leave whole. Add to the marinade. Marinate in the refrigerator overnight or at least 2 hours.

2 Boil or microwave the potatoes until tender. Drain. Cool slightly. Cut into bite-sized chunks.

3 To make the Concasse, if using, place the tomatoes, cilantro, onion, vinegar, oil, lemon juice, and black pepper to taste in a bowl. Mix to combine.

4 Preheat a barbecue hotplate or chargrill pan to very hot. Line a serving platter with the arugula leaves. Top with the potatoes, cucumber, and onions. Drain the octopus. Cook on the barbecue or in the pan, turning frequently, for 3–5 minutes or until the tentacles curl. Take care not to overcook or the octopus will be tough.

5 To serve, spoon the hot octopus over the prepared salad. Top with the concasse, if using. Accompany with crusty bread.

Serves 6

Crab Salad with Tomato Dressing

Ingredients

**2 large dressed crabs about
9 oz/255 g crabmeat**

**1 large bulb fennel, thinly sliced, and
feathery top chopped and
reserved to garnish**

3 oz/85 g mixed salad leaves

**1 tbsp snipped fresh chives
and paprika or cayenne pepper
to garnish**

Dressing

2 large tomatoes

5 tbsp olive oil

1 tbsp white wine vinegar

4 tbsp single cream

1 tsp chopped fresh tarragon

salt and black pepper

pinch of superfine sugar

dash of Worcestershire sauce

2 in/5 cm piece cucumber, diced

Method

1 To make the dressing, place the tomatoes in a bowl and cover with boiling water. Leave for 30 seconds, then skin, deseed, and cut into small dice. Whisk together the oil and vinegar in a bowl, then whisk in the cream, tarragon, and seasoning. Add the sugar and Worcestershire sauce to taste, then stir in the tomatoes and cucumber.

2 Mix together the crabmeat and sliced fennel and stir in 4 tablespoons of the dressing. Arrange the salad leaves together with the crab mixture on plates. Spoon over the remaining dressing, then sprinkle with the chives, chopped fennel top, and paprika or cayenne pepper.

Serves 4

73

Asparagus and Salmon Salad

Ingredients

1²/₃ lb/750 g asparagus spears, trimmed

lettuce leaves of your choice

18 oz/510 g smoked salmon slices

Lemon Yogurt Sauce:

1 cup plain low-fat yogurt

1 tbsp finely grated lemon rind

1 tbsp lemon juice

1 tbsp chopped fresh dill

1 tsp ground cumin

Method

1 Boil, steam or microwave the asparagus spears until tender. Drain, refresh under cold, running water, drain again and chill. Arrange the lettuce leaves, asparagus spears, and salmon on serving plates.

2 To make the Lemon Yogurt Sauce, place the yogurt, lemon rind, lemon juice, dill, and cumin in a small bowl and mix to combine.

3 Spoon the sauce over the salad, and cover and chill until required.

Note: If fresh asparagus spears are unavailable, green beans or snow peas are good alternatives for this recipe.

Serves 4

Rock Lobster and Smoked Ocean Trout Salad

Ingredients

2 lobster tails, cooked

14 oz/400 g smoked ocean trout

1 continental cucumber

1 carrot

1 green zucchini

1 yellow zucchini

3 1/2 oz/100 g arugula leaves

1 bunch chives, snipped

Dressing

juice of 2 limes

1 tbsp palm sugar
   or brown sugar

1/2 cup olive oil

salt and pepper

Method

1 Remove the meat from the lobster tails and slice finely. Cut the trout into thin strips. Place the lobster and trout in a container, cover, and refrigerate.

2 Wash the cucumber, slice in half lengthways, and scoop out and discard the seeds. Using a potato peeler or vegetable slicer, cut the cucumber and carrot into long thin ribbons. Cut the unpeeled green and yellow zucchini into long thin ribbons. Mix the lobster, ocean trout, ribboned vegetables, and arugulaleaves gently together in a large bowl.

3 In a bowl, place the lime juice and palm sugar. Heat in the microwave or over hot water to dissolve the sugar. Whisk in the olive oil, add the salt and pepper, and whisk until thick. Toss gently through the salad. Arrange the salad on an attractive platter and sprinkle over the chives.

serves 6

Seafood Paella Salad

Ingredients

4 cups chicken bouillon

I lb/455g uncooked jumbo shrimps

I uncooked lobster tail, optional

I lb/455 g mussels in shells, cleaned

2 tbsp olive oil

I onion, chopped

2 ham steaks, cut into I cm/¹/₂ in cubes

2 cups rice

¹/₂ tsp ground turmeric

4 oz/115 g fresh or frozen peas

I red bell pepper, diced

Garlic Dressing:

¹/₂ cup olive oil

¹/₄ cup white wine vinegar

3 tbsp mayonnaise

2 cloves garlic, crushed

2 tbsp chopped fresh parsley

freshly ground black pepper

Method

1 Place the bouillon in a large saucepan and bring to the boil. Add the jumbo shrimps and cook for 1–2 minutes or until they change color. Remove and set aside. Add the lobster tail and cook for 5 minutes or until the lobster changes color and is cooked. Remove and set aside. Add the mussels and cook until shells open, discarding any mussels that do not open after 5 minutes. Remove and set aside. Strain the bouillon and reserve. Peel and devein the shrimps, leaving the tails intact. Refrigerate the seafood until just prior to serving.

2 Heat the oil in a large saucepan, and add the onion and cook for 4–5 minutes or until soft. Add the ham, rice, and turmeric and cook, stirring, for 2 minutes. Add the reserved bouillon and bring to the boil. Reduce the heat, cover, and simmer for 15 minutes or until the liquid is absorbed and the rice is cooked and dry. Stir in the peas and red bell pepper and set aside to cool. Cover and refrigerate for at least 2 hours.

3 To make the Garlic Dressing, place the oil, vinegar, mayonnaise, garlic, parsley, and black pepper to taste in a food processor or blender and process to combine.

4 To serve, place the seafood and rice in a large salad bowl, spoon over the dressing, and toss to combine.

Serves 4

Tuna and Lemon Fettuccine Salad

Ingredients

1 lb/455g fettuccine

14 oz/400 g canned tuna in spring water, drained and flaked

7 oz/200 g arugula leaves, roughly chopped

5 oz/145 g reduced-fat feta cheese, chopped

1 tbsp chopped fresh dill

1/4 cup lemon juice

freshly ground black pepper

Method

1 Cook the fettuccine in boiling water in a large saucepan following the packet directions. Drain and return the pasta to the saucepan.

2 Place the saucepan over a low heat, and add the tuna, arugula, cheese, dill, lemon juice and black pepper to taste. Toss to combine, and serve immediately.

Serves 4

Mixed Shellfish and Potato Salad

Ingredients

1²/₃ lb/750 g waxy potatoes, unpeeled

salt

4 small cooked beetroot, diced

1 head fennel, finely sliced, plus
   feathery top, chopped

2¹/₄ lb/1 kg mussels

1 lb/455 g baby clams

1¹/₅ cups dry white wine or dry cider

1 shallot, finely chopped

4 scallions, finely sliced

3 tbsp chopped fresh parsley

Dressing

5 tbsp olive oil

1¹/₂ tbsp cider vinegar

¹/₂ tsp English mustard

salt and pepper to taste

Method

1 To make the dressing, whisk together the oil, vinegar, and mustard, and season to taste. Boil the potatoes in salted water for 15 minutes or until tender, then drain. Cool for 30 minutes, then peel and slice. Place in a bowl and toss with half the dressing. Toss the beetroot and fennel with the rest of the dressing.

2 Scrub the mussels and baby clams under cold, running water, pulling away any beards from the mussels. Discard any shellfish that are open or damaged. Place the wine or cider and shallot in a large saucepan and bring to the boil. Simmer for 2 minutes, then add the shellfish. Cover and cook briskly for 3–5 minutes, shaking the sauce pan often, or until opened. Discard any that remain closed. Reserve the pan juices, set aside a few mussels in their shells, and shell the rest.

3 Boil the pan juices for 5 minutes or until reduced to 1–2 tablespoons. Strain over the potatoes. Add the shellfish, scallions, and parsley, then toss. Serve with the beetroot and fennel salad and garnish with the fennel tops and mussels in their shells.

Serves 4

Shrimp and Pineapple Salad

Ingredients

10 water chestnuts, drained and chopped

1 tbsp grated green ginger

8 oz/225 g canned sliced pineapple, drained and cut into chunks

1 lb/455 g cooked shrimps, shelled

8 lettuce leaves, shaped like cups

3 scallions, sliced

1 tbsp sesame seeds, toasted lightly

Dressing

1 tbsp lemon juice

2 tbsp white wine vinegar

1 tbsp Dijon mustard

1/4 cup olive oil

2 tbsp sesame oil

Method

1 In a bowl, place the chopped water chestnuts, ginger, pineapple, and shrimps.

2 To make the dressing, whisk the lemon juice, vinegar, and mustard together, then gradually add the oils, whisking all the time until the dressing is thickened.

3 Add the dressing to the chestnut mixture and toss together lightly.

4 Arrange the salad lettuce cups, fill with the chestnut mixture, and garnish with scallions and sesame seeds.

Serves 4

Poultry can be roasted, but don't hesitate to use it in soups, stir-fries, salads, pâtés and dips. It goes with many flavors, including garlic, rosemary, lemons, chili, peas, soy sauce, and ginger. In this section, you will find many poultry recipes to tempt your family and friends.

Poultry

Poultry Appetizers

Thai Chicken Soup

Ingredients

2 cups low-salt chicken bouillon

2 kaffir lime or lemon myrtle leaves, optional

2 stalks fresh lemon grass or

2 tsp bottled lemon grass

1 bunchfresh cilantro with roots

5 thin slices fresh galangal or ginger

1 skinless chicken breast fillet, cut into thin strips

2 scallions, sliced

2 fresh bird's eye chilies or to taste

pinch sugar

2 tbsp rice wine (mirin) or sherry

juice of 1 lime

Method

1 Place the bouillon and lime leaves in a large saucepan. Bring to the boil.

2 Meanwhile, remove the outer layers from the lemon grass. Chop. Cut the roots from 2 of the cilantro plants. Chop. Remove leaves from the remaining cilantro. Set aside.

3 Place the lemon grass, cilantro roots and galangal in a mortar. Bruise with a pestle. Alternatively, place the ingredients in a plastic food bag and bruise with a rolling pin.

4 Stir the lemon grass mixture into the bouillon. Bring to simmering point, and simmer for 2–3 minutes. Add the chicken and scallions, and simmer for 5–6 minutes or until the chicken is cooked.

5 Place the reserved cilantro leaves, chilies, sugar, rice wine or sherry, and lime juice in a small bowl. Mix to combine.

6 To serve, divide the cilantro and chili mixture between warm soup bowls, and ladle over the soup. Mix gently to combine. For a main meal, serve with steamed jasmine rice.

Serves 2

Hot and Sour Chicken Soup

Ingredients

1¹/₃ lb/600 g chicken breast fillets
   (approximately 3)
2 tbsp peanut oil
4 cloves garlic, minced
2 shallots, chopped
5 stems of cilantro, leaves included
1 oz/30 g piece ginger, bruised
3 small red Thai chilies, ground
3 stalks lemon grass, finely sliced
6 kaffir lime leaves, finely shredded*
8 cups chicken or vegetable bouillon
3 tbsp Thai fish sauce*
3¹/₂ oz/100 g dry cellophane
   or glass noodles*
6 scallions, diagonally sliced
juice of 1–2 limes
handful of cilantro leaves

Method

1 Cut the chicken into ¹/₂ in/1 cm–thick strips. Brush the chicken strips with 1 tablespoon of peanut oil and broil or pan fry until the chicken is golden brown and slightly charred, about 3 minutes each side.

2 Heat the remaining tablespoon of peanut oil in a large saucepan, and add the garlic, shallots, chopped cilantro leaves and stems, ginger, ground chilies, sliced lemon grass, and finely shredded lime leaves and toss in the hot oil until fragrant, about 2 minutes. Add the bouillon and bring to the boil. Simmer for 10 minutes then add the broiled chicken strips and simmer for a further 10 minutes.

3 Add the Thai fish sauce and cellophone or grass noodles and simmer for a further 2 minutes, or until the noodles are tender.

4 Add the sliced scallions, lime juice, and cilantro leaves and serve very hot.

*Available from Asian grocers/foodstores

Serves 6

Moroccan Lemon Chicken Shish Kebabs

Ingredients

1 lb/455 g chicken breast fillets, trimmed of fat, cut into ¾ in/2 cm cubes

8 large metal or bamboo skewers

rice to serve

Moroccan Lemon Marinade:

1 tbsp chopped parsley

1 tbsp fresh rosemary leaves

2 tsp fresh thyme leaves

1 clove garlic, crushed

1 tsp black peppercorns, crushed

**grated rind (zest) and juice
  of 1 lemon**

1 tbsp olive oil

Method

1 To make the Moroccan Lemon Marinade,In a non-metallic bowl, place the parsley, rosemary, thyme, garlic, black pepper, lemon juice and rind, and oil. Add the chicken. Toss to combine. Cover and refrigerate for at least 30 minutes.

2 Preheat the barbecue or broiler to a high heat. If using bamboo skewers, soak in cold water for at least 20 minutes.

3 Thread the chicken onto the skewers. Place on the barbecue grill or under the broiler. Cook, brushing frequently with the marinade, and turn for 6–10 minutes or until the chicken is cooked. Serve on a bed of steamed rice.

Makes 8 shish kebabs

Chicken and Leek Soup with Herb Dumplings

Ingredients

**4 chicken thighs on the bone,
about 1³/₄ lb/800 g**

1 onion, chopped

1 carrot, chopped

**herb bundle made up of fresh
tarragon, parsley and a bay leaf**

4 tbsp butter

10 oz/285 g potatoes, cubed

3 large leeks, sliced

salt and black pepper

**2 chicken breast fillets, about
1 lb/455 g, cut into small strips**

2 tsp chopped fresh tarragon

**5 fl oz/145 mL light cream
herb dumplings**

**3¹/₂ oz/100 g all-purpose flour plus
¹/₂ tsp baking powder**

1¹/₂ tbsp fresh white breadcrumbs

¹/₄ cup shredded suet

**3 tbsp chopped fresh herbs
tarragon, parsley, or chives**

salt and pepper

Method

1 Place the chicken thighs, onion, carrot, and herb bundle in a large sauce pan with 6 cups of water. Simmer, covered, for 1 hour. Strain the bouillon and skim off any fat. Finely chop the chicken, discarding the skin and bones. Heat the butter in a separate large sauce pan. Add the potatoes and ²/₃ of the leeks, cover, and cook for 10 minutes. Pour in 4 cups of the bouillon and season. Simmer for 10–15 minutes, until softened. Blend until smooth in a food processor, return to the sauce pan, then stir in the cooked chicken. Set aside, and keep warm.

2 To make the dumplings, combine the flour, breadcrumbs, suet, herbs and seasoning in a large bowl. Stir in 4 tablespoons of water, mix well to combine, then shape into 8 dumplings. Cook in simmering salted water for 15–20 minutes.

3 Heat the remaining butter in a large frying pan. Cook the chicken breast for 4–5 minutes on each side. Add the remaining leek and cook for 2–3 minutes, until tender, then add to the soup with the tarragon and more bouillon, if necessary. Bring to the boil and simmer for 2 minutes. Remove from the heat and stir in the cream. Divide between 4 serving bowls. Drain the dumplings and add 2 to each bowl.

Serves 4

Chicken Minestrone

Ingredients

1 onion, finely chopped

1 clove garlic, chopped

1 stalk celery, diced

1 carrot, peeled and diced

14 oz/400 g can peeled tomatoes, no added salt

4 cups water

freshly ground black pepper

1 tsp dried oregano

1 tsp mixed spice

2 tbsp chopped parsley

1/2 cup cut macaroni

1/4 cabbage, shredded

1 cup frozen baby peas

7 oz/200 g chicken stirfry or chicken breast, chopped

crusty bread to serve

Method

1 Lightly spray base the of a large saucepan with a little olive oil spray. Add the onion and garlic, stirring over the heat until they color a little. Add the celery and carrot and continue to stir over the heat for 1 minute.

2 Chop the tomatoes and add to the saucepan with the juice. Stir in the water, pepper, oregano, spice, and parsley. Bring to the boil, and add the macaroni. Stir until the soup returns to the boil, turn down to a simmer, and cook for 15 minutes.

3 Stir in the cabbage, peas, and chicken stirfry. Simmer for 15–20 minutes. Serve hot with crusty bread.

Note: Left-over soup may be frozen for later use.

Serves 4–6

Chicken Cocktail Balls with Plum Sauce

Ingredients

1 lb/455 g ground chicken meat

10 shallots, finely chopped

¼ tsp five spice powder

1½ tbsp honey

1 tsp lemon zest

2 tbsp lemon juice

1½ cups fresh breadcrumbs

oil for frying

Plum Sauce

1 cup plum jelly

½ cup white vinegar

¼ tsp ground ginger

¼ tsp ground allspice

⅛ tsp hot chili powder

Method

1 In a food processor place all the chicken ball ingredients except the frying oil, and process together quickly. With wetted hands, shape into small balls. Place on a flat tray in a single layer and refrigerate for 30 minutes.

2 Heat the oil, at least 2 in/5 cm deep in a frying pan, or half full in a deep fryer, to 350°F/180°C. Deep-fry for about 3–4 minutes. Remove and drain on kitchen paper. Place a cocktail stick in each ball and arrange on a platter.

3 To make the Plum Sauce, place all the ingredients in a small saucepan and bring slowly to the boil while stirring. Simmer for 2 minutes. Remove from heat and cool. Pour into a small bowl and serve with the chicken balls.

Serves 4

Chicken Liver Pâté

Ingredients

9 oz/255 g chicken livers, cleaned

1 onion, peeled and quartered

1 clove garlic

1 strip bacon, cut into quarters

1/2 cup butter

1/2 tsp fresh thyme, chopped

salt and pepper

1 tbsp brandy

1/4 cup cream

1 packet water crackers

a little more thyme leaves to serve

Method

1 Place the onion, garlic, and bacon in a food processor and chop finely.

2 Melt the butter in a frying pan, add the bacon mixture and cook until tender. Add the chicken livers, thyme, salt and pepper. Cook a further 5 minutes.

3 Allow to cool slightly, then place back in the food processor and process until smooth.

4 Add the brandy and cream, and process until well combined.

5 Place into a large mould, surround with the water crackers and serve topped with the extra thyme leaves.

Makes about 1 lb/455 g

Pâté au Grand Marnier

Ingredients

6 1/2 oz/185 g butter

1 large onion, peeled and finely chopped

1 lb/455 g chicken livers, cleaned

2 tbsp Grand Marnier liqueur

salt and pepper

1 orange, sliced

1 packet water crackers

Method

1 Melt the half the butter in a frying pan, add the onion, and cook until soft.

2 Melt the remaining butter in the frying pan, add the chicken livers, and cook until brown on all sides, but still pink inside.

3 Place the cooked mixture into a food processor, add the Grand Marnier, salt, and pepper, and purée until smooth.

4 Place into 2 small serving bowls and refrigerate until set. Decorate with the orange slices.

5 Serve with the water crackers.

Makes about 1 2/3 lb/750g

Chicken and Rice Balls

Ingredients

I cup long grain rice

14 oz/400 g ground chicken

**³/₄ cup finely chopped
mushrooms**

**I small can water chestnuts,
drained and chopped finely**

3 scallions, sliced finely

I tsp finely chopped ginger

I tbsp soy sauce

2 egg whites

salt-reduced soy sauce to serve

Method

1 Cover the rice with cold water and leave for 2 hours, then drain well and place in a shallow dish.

2 Combine the remaining ingredients and form into small balls.

3 Roll the chicken balls in the rice so that the rice coats the entire surface.

4 Place the rice balls in the top part of a bamboo or stainless steel steamer so that they are not touching each other. Steam with the lid on for 15 minutes. Stand for 3–4 minutes. Serve with a small bowl of salt-reduced soy sauce for dipping.

Note: Batches of chicken and rice balls can be made in advance and stored in the refrigerator or freezer in plastic lock bags until required. This recipe is not suitable to microwave.

Makes 18

103

Chicken Empanadas

Ingredients

milk to glaze

Sour cream pastry
2¹/₂ cups all-purpose flour
pinch of salt
6 oz/170 g butter
1 egg
¹/₃ cup sour cream

Filling:
1¹/₂ tbsp butter or oil
1 onion, finely chopped
1 lb/455 g ground chicken
1 cup canned peach slices,
 chopped finely
salt and pepper

Method

1 Sift the flour and salt into a bowl, add the butter, and rub in with your fingertips until fine like breadcrumbs. Mix the egg and sour cream together, add to the flour mixture and mix to a dough. Wrap in plastic wrap and refrigerate for 30 minutes.

2 Heat the butter in a sauce pan, add the onion and sauté a few minutes. Add the ground chicken and stir while cooking until it changes color to white and then to a slightly golden color. Stir in the chopped peach, salt, and pepper. Allow to cool.

3 Roll out the dough between 2 sheets of baking paper. Remove the top sheet. Cut rounds of pastry about 4 x 4 in/10–12 cm in diameter. Place a heaped teaspoon of the filling in the center of each round, moisten the edges with water and fold over. Pinch the edges well together or press with the prongs of a fork. Glaze with the milk and bake in a preheated oven, 400°F/200°C/Gas Mark 6 for 10–15 minutes. Serve hot or cold as finger food, a snack, or a meal with vegetable accompaniments.

Makes 15–25

Lemon Chicken Fingers

Ingredients

2¼ lb/1 kg chicken breast fillets

oil for deep–frying

Marinade

2 tbsp soy sauce

¼ cup sherry

2 tsp grated fresh ginger

2 tsp lemon zest

2 tsp sugar

Batter

2 egg whites

¼ cup flour

¼ cup lemon juice

Dipping Sauce

reserved marinade

¼ cup chicken bouillon

2 tbsp lemon juice

2 tbsp cornstarch

Method

1 Cut the breast fillets into ½ in/1 cm wide strips from the long side of the fillet. Place the strips in a non-metal dish. Combine the marinade ingredients, pour over the strips, mix well, and allow to marinate for 30 minutes. Stiffly beat the egg whites to soft peak stage, and fold in the flour and lemon juice. Remove the strips from the marinade, reserving the marinade.

2 Heat the oil in a deep-fryer to 350°F/180°C. Dip a few strips at a time into the batter and deep-fry them for 5 minutes until golden. Drain on kitchen paper. Repeat with the remainder.

3 Pour the reserved marinade into a saucepan, add the chicken bouillon and bring to the boil. Mix to a smooth paste the lemon juice and cornstarch, stir into the saucepan, lower the heat, and stir until the sauce boils and thickens. Serve as finger food with the Dipping Sauce, or as a starter with the sauce and a salad garnish.

Serves 4

Chicken Yakitori

Ingredients

14 oz/400 g chicken stirfry
1/2 cup soy sauce
1/4 cup honey
1 clove garlic, crushed
1/2 tsp ground ginger
small bamboo skewers, soaked

Method

1 Place the chicken in a glass bowl, mix in the soy sauce, honey, garlic, and ginger. Cover, place in the refrigerator, and allow to marinate for several hours or overnight.

2 Thread one or two strips onto each skewer, using a weaving motion. Brush with the marinade.

3 Heat the broiler or barbecue to high. Grease the rack or plate with oil and arrange the skewers in a row. Cook for 2 1/2 minutes on each side, brushing with the marinade as they cook. Serve immediately.

Makes 25 small skewers (opposite)

Boston Wings

Ingredients

3 1/3 lb/1 1/2 kg chicken wings,
   tips discarded
3 tbsp butter
2 tbsp hot chili sauce
2 tbsp white vinegar
1/2 tsp paprika

Method

1 Arrange the chicken wings on a sheet of parchment placed on an oven tray. Bake in a medium hot oven at 350°F/180°C/Gas Mark 4 for about 40 minutes or until tender.

2 Heat the butter, chili sauce, vinegar, and paprika in a small saucepan and allow to simmer.

3 Take each chicken wing and hold over the saucepan while you brush each with the sauce. Place on a serving tray and keep warm. Serve immediately.

Makes about 40 wings

Tandoori Wings

Ingredients

24 chicken wings

lemon wedges to serve

yogurt with cucumber to serve

Marinade

7 oz/200 g tub reduced-fat yogurt

5 tbsp tandoori paste

2 tbsp dried coconut

Method

1 Combine the marinade ingredients and mix well. Marinate the chicken wings for at least 1 hour, ensuring each wing is well coated with the marinade.

2 Broil on high, turning occasionally, 2 in/5 cm from the heat source, or bake in the oven on a rack at 350°F/180°C/Mark 4 for 20–25 minutes.

3 Garnish with the lemon wedges and yogurt with cucumber.

Serves 4–6

Chicken Kebabs with Couscous

Ingredients

4 chicken breast fillets, skin off,
  cut into 24 pieces
1 yellow and 1 red bell pepper,
  deseeded and cut into 8 pieces
juice of 1 lemon
2 garlic cloves, crushed
2 tbsp extra virgin olive oil
1 tbsp chopped fresh cilantro
4 large wooden skewers

Sauce
3/5 cup yogurt
1 tbsp lemon juice
finely grated rind of 1/2 lemon
sea salt and freshly ground
  black pepper

Couscous
9 oz/255 g couscous
1 oz/30 g butter
4 scallions, finely chopped
3 tbsp chopped fresh cilantro

Method

1 Place the chicken and bell peppers in a non-metallic bowl, add the lemon juice, garlic, olive oil, and cilantro and mix. Cover and leave to marinate for at least 1 hour. Meanwhile, combine all the ingredients for the sauce. Season with salt and pepper and leave to chill. Soak 4 large wooden skewers in water for about 10 minutes.

2 Preheat the grill to high. Thread the chicken and bell peppers onto the skewers and grill for 10–12 minutes, turning occasionally, until the chicken is slightly charred, cooked through, and tender. Keep warm.

3 Meanwhile, prepare the couscous according to packet instructions, then fluff up with a fork. Melt the butter in a small saucepan and fry the scallions for about 2 minutes. Add the scallions with 3 tablespoons of cilantro and plenty of seasoning to the couscous and mix well. Serve the couscous on plates, with the kebabs on top, then drizzle with the yogurt sauce.

Note: The lemony marinade infuses the chicken and peppers with its lovely flavor and tenderizes the meat. Marinate overnight if possible.

Serves 4

Crispy Drumsticks

Ingredients

2 1/4 lb/1 kg chicken drumsticks

4 tbsp seasoned flour

2 eggs, lightly beaten

1 tbsp milk

3 oz/85 g packet potato chips

2 cups cornflakes

Method

1 Wipe over the drumsticks with kitchen towel.

2 Place the seasoned flour on a sheet of kitchen paper. Beat the eggs and milk together in a flat dish. Crush the chips and cornflakes together with a rolling pin, and place on kitchen paper. Dip the drumsticks in the flour, then the egg mixture, and then in the crumb mixture. Press on the crumbs firmly.

3 Place the drumsticks on a wire rack over a baking dish. Place in a preheated oven for 45–50 minutes until golden and cooked through.

4 Serve the drumsticks hot with assorted vegetable sticks and a mayonnaise dip.

Serves 6–8

Chunky Chicken Dip

Ingredients

1 cup cooked finely chopped chicken

¼ cup chopped almonds

¼ cup chopped celery

¼ cup chopped chives

¼ cup mayonnaise

¼ cup sour cream

salt and pepper to taste

Method

1 Combine all the ingredients together. Mix well.

2 Serve with a selection of water crackers.

Serves 4–6

Potted Chicken

Ingredients

2 cups ground cooked chicken

1 small onion, very finely chopped

2 hard–boiled eggs, mashed

2 tbsp brandy

⅓ cup mayonnaise

dash Tabasco

salt and pepper

Method

1 Combine all the ingredients. Pack into a serving dish and refrigerate.

2 Serve with a selection of water crackers.

Serves 4–6

Chicken and Prune Roll

Ingredients

2 bacon strips, finely chopped

1 medium onion, finely chopped

5 pitted prunes, chopped

1 lb/455 g ground chicken

2 tbsp dried breadcrumbs

$1/2$ tsp salt

$1/2$ tsp pepper

1 tsp cumin

1 egg, lightly beaten

1 sheet frozen puff pastry

5 pitted whole prunes

1 tbsp milk

2 tsp poppy seeds

Method

1 In a small heated pan, place the bacon and onion and cook while stirring for 1 minute. Mix the chopped prunes, ground chicken, breadcrumbs, salt, pepper, cumin, egg, and the bacon and onion mixture. Combine well.

2 Preheat the oven to 400°F/200°C/Gas Mark 6. Line a flat oven tray with a sheet of baking paper and place the sheet of thawed puff pastry onto the tray. Spoon $1/2$ of the chicken mixture along the center of the sheet in an even strip about 3 in/8 cm wide and to the edge of the pastry at both ends. Arrange the 5 whole prunes along the center then cover with the remaining chicken mixture and smooth to an even thickness.

3 Brush the back strip of the pastry with water, lift the front pastry over the chicken mixture and lift the back pastry to overlap the front. Press lightly along the seam to seal. Lift the paper and turn the chicken roll over to rest on the seam join. Pull the paper to bring it into the center of the tray, and trim off the paper overhang. Glaze the roll with the milk and sprinkle with the poppy seeds.

4 Bake in the oven for 15 minutes. Turn the oven down to 350°F/180°C/Gas Mark 4, and continue cooking for 25 minutes until golden. Slice and serve.

Curried Chicken Rolls

Ingredients

2 tbsp canola oil

1 medium onion, finely chopped

1 small clove garlic, crushed

2 tsp mild curry paste

1 1/2 tbsp lemon juice

1 lb/455 g ground chicken

3 tbsp dried breadcrumbs

1/2 tsp salt

1/2 tsp pepper

2 tbsp chopped fresh cilantro

2 sheets frozen puff pastry, thawed

1 tbsp milk for glazing

1 tbsp sesame seeds

Method

1 Heat the oil in a small sauce pan, add the onion and garlic, and fry until the onion is soft. Stir in the curry paste and cook a little. Add the lemon juice and stir to mix. In a bowl, combine the chicken, breadcrumbs, salt, pepper and cilantro. Add the onion and curry mixture and combine well.

2 Preheat the oven to 370°F/190°C/Gas Mark 5. Cut each sheet of puff pastry in 1/2 across the center. Pile a 1/4 of the chicken mixture in a thick 1/2 in/1 1/2 cm wide strip along the center of each pastry strip. Brush the exposed pastry at the back with water.

3 Lift the front strip of the pastry over the filling and roll to rest onto the back strip. Press lightly to seal.

4 Cut the roll into 4 or 5 equal portions. Repeat the process with the remaining chicken mixture and pastry.

5 Glaze with the milk and sprinkle with the sesame seeds. Place onto a flat baking tray. Cook in the preheated oven for 10 minutes, reduce the heat to 350°F/180°C/Gas Mark 4, and continue cooking for 15 minutes until golden brown. Serve hot as finger food.

Serves 4–6

Chicken and Almond Triangles

Ingredients

1 tbsp olive oil

1/4 cup slivered almonds

1 medium onion, finely chopped

1/4 tsp salt

1 tsp ground cinnamon

1 tsp paprika

2 tsp ground cumin

1 lb/455 g ground chicken

2 small tomatoes, chopped

1 1/2 oz/45 g raisins, chopped

2 tbsp finely chopped Italian parsley

4 tbsp dry white wine

14 sheets filo pastry

canola oil spray

Method

1 Heat a heavy-based frying pan. Add 1 teaspoon of the oil and sauté the almonds until pale gold in color. Quickly remove with a slotted spoon. Add the remaining oil and the onion and fry until soft. Stir in the salt, cinnamon, paprika and cumin and cook until aromatic. Add the ground chicken and stir fry until almost cooked. Add the tomatoes, raisins, parsley, wine, and cooked almonds. Simmer, covered, for 15 minutes. Uncover and cook until the juices are absorbed. Allow to cool.

2 Position the pastry with the long side in front of you. Cut into 3 even 5 1/4 in/13 1/2 cm wide strips. Stack and cover with a clean kitchen towel. Take 2 strips at a time, spray each lightly with the canola oil spray, and fold in half, long side to long side. Spray the surface with the oil spray.

3 Place 1/2 teaspoon of the filling on the bottom end of each strip. Fold the right-hand corner over to form a triangle, then fold on the straight, then on diagonal until the end is reached. Repeat with the remaining. Place on a tray sprayed with the oil. Spray the tops of the triangles with the oil and bake in a preheated moderate oven 350°F/180°C/Gas Mark 4 for 20–25 minutes. Serve hot as finger food.

Makes 42

Middle Eastern Chicken Pasties

Ingredients

1 quantity Ricotta Pastry
milk

Chicken and Vegetable Filling:
1 tsp olive oil
1 small red onion, diced
1 stalk celery, diced
1 tsp ground cumin
1/2 tsp dry mustard
1 1/4 cups skinless shredded
   cooked chicken
1/2 cup grated zucchini or chopped
   green bell pepper
1/2 cup additional vegetables
   (e.g. chopped spinach or grated
   pumpkin)
2 tbsp currants or golden raisins
1 tbsp chopped fresh parsley
   or oregano
1/4 cup low-fat plain yogurt
1 tbsp chutney
2 tbsp couscous
1 tsp grated lemon zest
2 tsp lemon juice

Ricotta Pastry
2 cups all-purpose flour
2 tsp baking soda
1/2 cup low-fat ricotta cheese
1/2 cup buttermilk
1 egg white
2 tbsp unsaturated oil
1–2 tbsp chilled skim milk

Method

1 To make the Filling, heat the oil in a nonstick frying pan over a medium heat. Add the onion, celery, cumin, and mustard. Cook, stirring, for 2–3 minutes or until soft and fragrant.

2 Add the chicken, zucchini, additional vegetables, currants, parsley, yogurt, and chutney. Cook, stirring occasionally, for 5–7 minutes. Remove the pan from the heat. Stir in the couscous, lemon zest, and lemon juice. Cool.

3 Preheat the oven. Lightly spray or brush a baking tray with unsaturated oil or line with nonstick baking paper.

4 To make the pastry, place the flour, ricotta cheese, buttermilk, egg white, and oil in a food processor. Using the pulse button, process until just combined. With the machine running, slowly add the skim milk until the mixture forms a dough. Turn the pastry onto a lightly floured surface. Knead into a ball. Wrap the pastry in plastic wrap. Refrigerate for at least 30 minutes or until ready to use.

5 To assemble, roll out the pastry to 1/8 in/2 mm thick and, using a bread and butter plate as a guide, cut out 4 rounds. Place 1/4 of the filling on 1 half of each round, leaving a 1/2 in/1 cm border around the edge. Brush the edge with the milk or water. Fold the uncovered half over the filling, pressing the edges to seal. Using a fork, prick the pastry several times. Place on a prepared baking tray. Brush with milk. Bake for 20 minutes at 370°F/190°C/Gas Mark 5 or until the pastry is crisp and golden.

Makes 4 pasties

Poultry Mains

Thigh Steaks with Fruity Mint Salsa

Ingredients

1 lb/455g chicken thighs

canola oil spray

salt and pepper to taste, optional

1/2 tsp dried oregano

1 pear, peeled and diced

1 banana, peeled and diced

2 tbsp lemon juice

3 tbsp finely chopped mint

2 tbsp sweet chili sauce

mashed potatoes or rice to serve

Method

1 Pound the thigh fillets on both sides with a meat mallet to flatten. Sprinkle with salt, if using, pepper, and oregano.

2 Heat a non-stick frying pan and lightly spray with oil, place in the thigh steaks, and cook for 3 minutes on each side. Remove to a heated plate and keep hot. Add the diced pear, banana, lemon juice, mint and chili sauce to the pan. Scrape up the pan juices and stir to heat the fruit.

3 Pile the hot fruit salsa on top of the thigh steaks. Serve immediately with the mashed potatoes or rice.

Serves 3–4

Drumsticks in Dill Sauce

Ingredients

2 tbsp butter

2¼ lb/1 kg chicken drumsticks

1 cup chopped scallions

3 tbsp finely chopped dill

¼ cup lemon juice

½ tsp salt

¼ tsp white pepper

1 bunch Dutch carrots, peeled

2 cups water

1 chicken bouillon cube

2 tbsp cornstarch

2 tbsp water

crusty bread to serve

Method

1 Heat the butter in a wide-based saucepan. Add the drumsticks a few at a time and brown lightly on all sides. Remove to a plate and brown the remainder.

2 Add the scallions and sauté for 1 minute. Stir in the chopped dill. Add the lemon juice, return the drumsticks to the saucepan, and sprinkle with the salt and pepper.

3 Arrange the carrots over the drumsticks. Add the water and bouillon cube. Bring to a simmer, turn down the heat, cover, and simmer for 40 minutes until tender.

4 Remove the drumsticks and carrots with a slotted spoon and arrange on a heated platter.

5 Blend the cornstarch with the water, and stir into the juices remaining in the pan. Stir over the heat until the sauce boils and thickens. Pour over the drumsticks and carrots. Serve immediately with crusty bread.

Serves 6

Apricot Glazed Chicken with Savory Stuffing

Ingredients

3 lb/1 1/3 kg fresh chicken

1 tbsp soy sauce

1/2 lemon

1 tbsp flour, for gravy

Apricot Dipping Sauce

1/2 cup apricot jelly

1 tbsp soy sauce

1 tbsp lemon juice

2 tbsp white vinegar

1 tbsp water

Easy Stuffing

3–4 bacon strips, chopped

1 large onion, finely chopped

1 1/2 cups long grain rice, rinsed

3 cups boiling water

2 tsp soy sauce

2 tsp mixed dried herbs

2 tbsp chopped parsley

Method

1 To make the Apricot Dipping Sauce, mix all the sauce ingredients together and heat gently while stirring.

2 Prepare the chicken for roasting. Mix together the Apricot Dipping Sauce and the soy sauce, and brush over the chicken and inside the cavity. Place the lemon half in the cavity. Place the chicken on an adjustable rack, breast-side down. Add 1 cup of water to the dish, and cook in a preheated oven at 350°F/180°C/Gas Mark 4 for 40 minutes. Brush again with the sauce and turn breast-side up, brush with the sauce, and cook for 40–50 minutes more, until cooked when tested.

3 When the chicken is placed in the oven, prepare the stuffing. Place all the ingredients in a lidded casserole dish and place on a shelf in the oven under the chicken. Cook for 40 minutes, then remove from the oven, and stand, covered for 10 minutes. When the chicken is cooked, remove from the dish and cover with foil to rest. Skim the fat from roasting the pan and add about 1 cup of water to dissolve any cooked-on pan juices. Pour into a small saucepan. Add the flour blended with a little water and stir until it thickens and boils.

4 Carve the chicken and serve with the stuffing, gravy, and vegetable accompaniments.

Serves 4

Citrus and Spice Grilled Chicken

Ingredients

2¼ lb/1 kg chicken

Marinade
½ cup cider vinegar

½ cup orange juice

½ cup grapefruit juice

1 tsp cinnamon

½ tsp ground nutmeg

1 tsp sugar

½ tsp salt optional

Method

1 Wash the chicken inside and out and pat dry with kitchen towel. With a cleaver or large sharp knife, cut the chicken through the breastbone and open out. Cut on each side of the backbone and discard.

2 Mix the marinade ingredients together. Place the chicken halves in a non-metal dish and smother with the marinade. Cover and refrigerate for 12 hours or overnight, turning occasionally.

3 Heat the oven griller element or broiler to medium. Place the chicken halves in the base of the grill pan under the grill. Cook for 10 minutes on each side brushing frequently with marinade.

4 Lift the chicken onto the grilling rack so as to come closer to heat and cook 5 minutes on each side. Turn the heat to high and cook about 2 minutes to brown and crisp. Remove the chicken to a heated platter.

5 Skim the fat from the pan juices and pour the juices over the chicken. Serve hot with vegetable accompaniments.

Serves 2–3

Grilled Sesame Chicken with Ginger Rice

Ingredients

1 lb/455 g skinless chicken breast or thigh fillets or tenderloin, trimmed of visible fat

Soy and Honey Marinade

1 tbsp sesame seeds, toasted

1 tbsp rice wine (mirin) or sherry

2 tsp honey or plum sauce

2 tsp reduced-salt soy sauce

2 tsp oyster sauce

1 tsp sesame oil

Ginger Rice

1 tbsp finely chopped fresh ginger

1 tsp sesame oil

1 cup short or medium grain rice, rinsed and drained

$1^2/_5$ cups ginger beer

1 tbsp diced pickled or preserved ginger

1 tbsp finely chopped scallions, optional

Method

1 To make the Soy and Honey Marinade, place the sesame seeds, wine, sauces, and sesame oil in a non-reactive bowl. Mix to combine.

2 Cut the chicken into large pieces. Add to the marinade. Toss to coat. Cover. Marinate in the refrigerator for at least 1 hour.

3 To make the rice, place the fresh ginger and sesame oil in a large saucepan over a low heat. Cook, stirring occasionally, for 5 minutes. Add the rice. Cook, stirring, for 2 minutes. Stir in the ginger beer and pickled ginger. Bring to the boil. Reduce the heat. Cover. Steam for 10–15 minutes or until the liquid is absorbed and the rice is cooked. Stir in the scallions.

4 Meanwhile, preheat the broiler or barbecue to a medium heat. Drain the chicken. Cook under the broiler or on the barbecue, brushing occasionally with the marinade, for 6–7 minutes or until cooked through and slightly crispy on the outside. The chicken is cooked when the juices run clear when pressed with a fork. Serve the chicken with the Ginger Rice and steamed Napa cabbage.

Serves 4

Malaysian Grilled Chicken

Ingredients

4 skinless chicken breasts on the bone

2 tsp cornstarch blended with 2 tbsp water cucumber slices

red bell pepper strips, optional

Spicy Oriental Marinade

1 red onion, quartered

2 cloves garlic, chopped

1 tbsp grated fresh ginger

1 tbsp ground cilantro

1 tbsp palm sugar, crumbled, or brown sugar

1 tsp Chinese five spice powder

1/4 cup rice wine (mirin)

1/4 cup orange or lime juice

1 tbsp reduced-salt thick dark soy sauce

Method

1 To make the Spicy Oriental Marinade, place the onion and garlic in a food processor. Process to chop finely. Transfer to a bowl. Add the ginger, cilantro, sugar, five spice powder, wine, orange juice, and soy sauce. Mix to combine.

2 Place the chicken in a shallow glass or ceramic dish. Pour over the marinade. Turn to coat. Cover. Marinate in the refrigerator overnight. Transfer the chicken and marinade to a large nonstick frying pan.

3 Place the pan over a medium heat. Bring to the boil. Reduce the heat. Simmer for 15–20 minutes or until chicken is just tender; take care not to overcook. Using a slotted spoon, remove the chicken from the cooking liquid. Place in a clean dish. Cover. Refrigerate until ready to barbecue or stir fry. Reserve the marinade.

4 Preheat the barbecue to a medium heat. Cook the chicken on the barbecue grill for 5 minutes each side or until richly colored and heated through. Alternatively, heat a little oil in a wok over a high heat. Add the chicken. Stir fry for 3–4 minutes or until heated through.

5 Place the reserved marinade and the cornstarch mixture in a small saucepan over a medium heat. Cook, stirring constantly, for 4–5 minutes or until the sauce boils and thickens.

6 To serve, spoon the sauce over the chicken and accompany with the cucumber and red bell pepper, if using.

Serves 4

Chicken Breasts with Shiitake Mushrooms

Ingredients

2 tbsp groundnut oil

I onion, chopped

2 in/5 cm piece fresh root ginger, finely chopped

7 oz/200 g shiitake mushrooms, stems removed and caps sliced

5 oz/145 g baby button mushrooms

2 tbsp dark soy sauce

I cup chicken bouillon

I cup white wine

12 oz/340 g patty pan squash, halved, or zucchini, trimmed and sliced

6 skinless boneless chicken breasts

chopped fresh cilantro to garnish

noodles to serve

Method

I Preheat the oven. Heat I tablespoon of the oil in a large, heavy-based saucepan, add the onion and the ginger, and fry for 5 minutes or until the onion has softened. Add the shiitake and button mushrooms and the soy sauce and cook for a further 4–5 minutes, until the mushrooms have softened.

2 Stir in the bouillon and wine, bring to the boil, then simmer for I0 minutes. Add the squash or zucchini and cook for a further 5 minutes or until tender.

3 Meanwhile, make 3 slashes in each chicken breast, using a sharp knife. Heat the remaining oil in a large, heavy-based frying pan, add the chicken, and fry for 2–3 minutes each side to brown.

4 Transfer the chicken to an ovenproof dish and spoon over the mushroom mixture. Bake for I5–20 minutes at 450°F/230°C/Gas Mark 8, until the chicken is cooked through. Sprinkle with the cilantro just before serving with noodles.

Serves 6

Risotto of Indian Spiced Chicken with Chickpeas

Ingredients

3 cloves garlic, crushed

2 tsp ground cumin

2 tsp paprika

2 tsp ground cilantro

1 tbsp Garam Masala

1 tsp ground ginger

3 tbsp mango or apricot chutney

juice and zest of 1 orange

4 tbsp olive oil

4 boneless, skinless thigh fillets cut into strips, or 12 'winglets'

1 tbsp ghee

1 bunch scallions, trimmed and chopped

14 oz/400 g arborio rice

4 cups well-flavored vegetable bouillon

14 oz/400 g can chickpeas, drained and rinsed

2 handfuls baby spinach, washed

4 oz/115 g golden raisins

2 tbsp yogurt, optional

2 tbsp fresh mint, chopped

salt and freshly ground pepper

4 oz/115 g toasted almonds

Method

1   In a glass jug, mix together the garlic, cumin, paprika, cilantro, Garam Marsala, ginger, chutney, orange juice and zest, and oil. Mix very well, then pour over the chicken in a non-reactive baking dish (glass or ceramic) and allow to marinate for 6 hours overnight.

2   In a saucepan, heat the ghee and add 1/2 the scallions and cook gently until softened. Remove the chicken from the marinade and add to the scallions, cooking until the chicken begins to change color, about 3 minutes.

3   Remove the chicken from the pan, add the rice and begin adding the bouillon, 1/2 a cup at a time and allowing each to be absorbed before the next quantity of bouillon is added. When adding the last of the bouillon, add the chickpeas, baby spinach, and golden raisins and mix vigorously to incorporate. When the liquid has been absorbed, remove the saucepan from the heat and add the remaining scallions, yogurt, if using, fresh mint, and salt and pepper to taste. Serve immediately, garnished with the almonds.

Note: The aromatic spices that marinate the chicken create delicious musky flavors that permeate the rice. The chicken will benefit from a marination of at least 6 hours, but if time is scarce, 1–2 hours will do.

Serves 6

Chicken Cannelloni

Ingredients

2 tbsp olive oil

I onion, finely chopped

I lb/455 g ground chicken

3 rashes bacon. ground

salt and pepper

cannelloni tubes

butter for greasing pan

I cup tomato pasta sauce

1/2 cup water

Bechamel Sauce

6 oz/170 g butter

3/4 cup flour

4 cups milk

1/8 tsp nutmeg

3 tbsp grated Parmesan cheese

2 eggs, beaten

salt and pepper for seasoning

extra Parmesan cheese to sprinkle

2 tsp butter

Method

1 Heat the olive oil in a large sauce pan, add the onion, and sauté for 2 minutes, then add the ground chicken and bacon and stir until browned and cooked. Remove from the heat and season to taste. Set aside.

2 To make Bechamel Sauce, melt the butter in a saucepan, add the flour and stir I minute. Remove from the heat, gradually add the milk, stirring well. Return to the heat, stirring until the sauce thickens and boils. Remove from the heat, stir in the nutmeg, cheese and eggs. Season to taste.

3 Fill the cannelloni tubes with the chicken mixture. Grease a large oven dish. Mix the pasta sauce and water together and spread 1/2 over the base of the dish. Place cannelloni tubes in two rows in the dish then pour over remaining pasta sauce. Pour over the bechamel sauce, spread evenly and sprinkle with a little grated Parmesan cheese. Dot with 2 teaspoons butter and bake in preheated oven 180°C/350°F/Gas Mark 4 for 30–35 minutes until golden brown. Serve hot with a tossed salad.

Serves 6

Oven-Baked Parmesan Chicken

Ingredients

**1 oz/30 g fresh breadcrumbs, made
from 1 slice stonebaked white loaf,
crusts removed**

**3 oz/85 g Parmesan cheese,
finely grated**

2 scallions, finely chopped

**finely grated zest and juice of
1/2 lemon**

2 oz/55 g butter, melted

**sea salt and freshly ground black
pepper**

4 skinless chicken breast fillets

2 tbsp chopped fresh parsley

Method

1 Preheat the oven to 375°F/190°C/Gas Mark 5.
Mix the breadcrumbs, Parmesan, scallions, lemon
zest, butter, and seasoning together in a small bowl.
Divide the mixture between the chicken breasts
and, using a fork, press the mixture down on top,
to form an even coat.

2 Transfer the chicken breasts to a shallow
roasting tin and bake for 20 minutes. Remove the
chicken from the roasting tin and keep warm. Add
the lemon juice and parsley to the buttery juices in
the tin and mix well. Pour these juices over the
chicken, and serve immediately.

Serves 4

Roasted Herby Chicken with Pears

Ingredients

juice of 2 lemons

salt and black pepper

12 chicken drumsticks, skinned

6 firm pears, peeled, halved, cored and cut crossways into $^1/_2$ in/1 cm slices

$^3/_5$ cup white wine

1 tbsp chopped fresh thyme or 1 tsp dried thyme

1 tbsp chopped fresh tarragon

1 tbsp chopped fresh rosemary

Method

1 Mix together the lemon juice and seasoning. Put the drumsticks into a shallow, non-metallic bowl, pour over the seasoned lemon juice, and rub into the skin with your fingertips. Cover and marinate in the fridge for 30 minutes.

2 Meanwhile, preheat the oven to 400°F/200°C/ Gas Mark 6. Arrange the pears in a deep ovenproof dish, then top with the chicken and pour over the marinating juices. Pour over the wine and sprinkle with the thyme, tarragon, and rosemary. Cover the dish with foil.

3 Cook for 1 hour, basting 1–2 times, until the chicken is tender. Remove the foil and increase the oven temperature to 450°F/230°C/Gas Mark 8. Cook for a further 10 minutes or until the chicken is cooked through and the skin has browned. Leave it to rest, covered, for 10 minutes before serving.

Serves 6

Spanish Chicken with Chorizo

Ingredients

**8 chicken joints, such as thighs
  and drumsticks**

2 tbsp olive oil

I onion, sliced

2 cloves garlic, crushed

**I red and I yellow bell pepper,
  deseeded and sliced**

2 tsp paprika

1/4 cup dry sherry or dry vermouth

14 oz/400 g can chopped tomatoes

I bay leaf

**I strip orange rind, pared
  with a vegetable peeler**

2 1/2 oz/70 g chorizo, sliced

1/4 cup pitted black olives

salt and black pepper

Method

I Place the chicken joints in a large non stick frying pan and fry without oil for 5–8 minutes, turning occasionally, until golden. Remove the chicken and set aside, then pour away any fat from the pan.

2 Add the oil to the frying pan and fry the onion, garlic and bell pepper for 3–4 minutes, until softened. Return the chicken to the pan with the paprika, sherry or vermouth, tomatoes, bay leaf, and orange rind. Bring to the boil, then simmer, covered, over a low heat for 35–40 minutes, stirring occasionally, until the chicken is cooked through.

3 Add the chorizo and olives, and simmer for a further 5 minutes to heat through, then season with the salt and pepper.

Serves 4

Chicken with Saffron Rice and Peas

Ingredients

3 lb/1¹/₃ kg chicken, cut into 6–8
    serving pieces

freshly ground black pepper

2 tbsp oil

4 oz/115 g salt pork or spek, finely diced

2 red onions, sliced

1 tsp finely chopped garlic

2¹/₂ tsp paprika

1 medium-sized tomato, finely chopped

1¹/₄ cups uncooked rice

5 oz/145 g fresh or frozen peas

3 cups boiling water

¹/₈ tsp ground saffron or
    1 tsp turmeric

2 tbsp finely chopped parsley

Method

1 Pat the chicken pieces dry with kitchen paper and sprinkle with a few grindings of pepper.

2 Heat the oil over a moderate heat in a heavy frying pan. Add the diced salt pork or spek and cook, stirring, until brown and crisp. Remove the pork with a slotted spoon and drain on kitchen paper.

3 Add the chicken to the pan and brown evenly on all sides. Set the chicken aside.

4 Pour off all but a little oil and fat from the pan. Stir in the onions and garlic and cook for about 5 minutes, until the onions are soft and transparent. Stir in the paprika, then the tomato and bring to the boil, stirring frequently. Cook briskly, uncovered, for about 5 minutes until most of the liquid inthe pan has evaporated.

5 Return the chicken and pork to the pan. Add the rice, peas, boiling water, and saffron or turmeric, and stir well to combine. Bring quickly to the boil and reduce the heat to low. Cover and simmer for 20–30 minutes until the chicken and rice are tender and all the liquid is absorbed. Taste and adjust the seasoning. Sprinkle with the parsley and serve.

Serves 6

Chicken in Garlic Sauce

Ingredients

3 1/3 lb/ 1 1/2 kg chicken, cut into small
    serving pieces (split the breast and
    cut in half again, cut each thigh
    in half)

salt

5 tbsp olive oil

6 cloves garlic, chopped, plus 1 clove,
    ground

1 tbsp ground parsley

2 tbsp dry white wine

Method

1 Sprinkle the chicken with the salt. Heat the oil in a shallow flameproof casserole, and brown the chicken over a medium-high heat on all sides. Add the chopped garlic, reduce the heat to medium and cook, stirring occasionally, for 30 minutes.

2 Stir in the ground garlic, parsley, and wine. Cover and cook for 15 minutes more, or until the chicken is done and the juices run clear when the thigh is pricked with a fork. Serve with vegetables.

Serves 4

Sweet and Sour Chicken Noodles

Ingredients

1 carrot, sliced

1 red bell pepper

1 green bell pepper

2 stalks celery, sliced

1/2 tin baby corn, sliced

1/2 tin water chestnuts

2 tbsp oil

14oz/400g chicken fillets, sliced

3oz /85g boiled noodles

Sweet and Sour Sauce

2 tbsp sugar

3 tbsp vinegar

1 1/4 cup pineapple juice

1 tsp tomato paste

1 tsp ginger, crushed

1 clove garlic, crushed

Method

1 To make the Sweet and Sour Sauce, brown the sugar in a sauce pan, add the vinegar, pineapple juice, tomato paste, ginger, and crushed garlic. Simmer for 2 minutes, then remove from heat and set aside.

2 Stir fry the vegetables and chestnuts in a hot wok for 1–2 minutes, remove, and set aside. Add a little oil to the wok and cook the chicken. When the chicken is cooked, add the sauce, vegetables, and noodles, and cook for 2 minutes.

Squab with Almonds and Pine Nuts

Ingredients

4 small poussins

salt and freshly ground black pepper

olive oil to brush

4 small lemon wedges

4 bay leaves

2 tablespoons olive oil

1 medium onion, thinly sliced

3 cloves garlic, crushed

1 lb/455g tomatoes, skinned, de-seeded
   and roughly chopped

¹/₂ cup red wine

2 tablespoons sun-dried tomato paste

1 green chili, de-seeded and
   thinly sliced

1 medium red bell pepper,
   cut into thin strips

1 small green bell pepper,
   cut into thin strips

3 tablespoons blanched almonds,
   chopped

1 tablespoon pine nuts

12 pitted black olives

2 tablespoons sultanas or raisins

Method

1   Preheat the oven to 375°F/190°C/Gas Mark 5.
Rub poussins with salt and pepper, inside and
out. Brush the skins with olive oil and stuff a
lemon wedge and bay leaf inside each one.
Roast for about 45 minutes, until tender.

2   Meanwhile, heat olive oil in a large frying
pan, and sauté onion and garlic until
translucent. Add tomatoes and fry lightly for a
further 2 minutes. Add all remaining ingredients
and simmer for 20–25 minutes, until sauce has
thickened and tomatoes are soft.

3   Place poussins on a serving dish and spoon the
sauce over. Serve with remaining sauce in a jug.
Serves 4

Poultry Salads

Party Avocado and Chicken Salad

Ingredients

2¼ lb/1 kg chicken breast fillets

3 avocados

1 tbsp lemon juice

2 stalks celery, thinly sliced

¼ cup slivered almonds, toasted

½ green bell pepper, cut into slices

**14 oz/400 g can mango slices, drained
   or fresh mango in season**

1 cucumber, peeled deseeded and diced

lettuce to serve

Dressing:

1 cup thickened cream, whipped

½ cup mayonnaise

½ tsp grated nutmeg

1 tsp paprika

salt and pepper

Method

1 Poach the chicken. Cool, then cut into large dice ½ in–1 in/1½–2½ cm. Peel and slice the avocado, and sprinkle with the lemon juice.

2 Combine the chicken, celery, almonds, bell pepper, and most of the avocado, mango slices, and cucumber.

3 Mix the cream, mayonnaise, and spices together to make the dressing, then pour over the salad and toss gently. Arrange the lettuce leaves on a shallow platter, and pile on the chicken mixture. Garnish with the reserved avocado, mango, and cucumber.

Serves 10–20

Chicken Caesar Salad

Ingredients

2 chicken breast fillets

1 clove garlic, crushed

salt and pepper

2 tsp olive oil

1 tbsp lemon juice

1 Romaine lettuce

$1/4$ cup grated Parmesan cheese

1 cup garlic croutons

shaved Parmesan cheese to garnish

Dressing

2 anchovy fillets

4 tbsp olive oil

$2^1/2$ tbsp lemon juice

$1/2$ tsp salt

$1/4$ tsp pepper

1 coddled egg

pinch of dry mustard

1 tsp Worcestershire sauce

Method

1 Trim the chicken fillets. Mix together the garlic, salt, pepper, oil, and lemon juice, and cover and marinate the chicken for 30 minutes in the refrigerator. Heat the grill or chargrill until hot. Sear the fillets 1 minute on each side, then cook 3 minutes each side. Remove and rest for 5 minutes before cutting into $1/5$ in/$1/2$ cm slices on the diagonal.

2 Separate the leaves of the lettuce, discard the outer leaves and wash well. Drain and shake dry in a clean kitchen towel. Cut the greener leaves into bite-sized pieces and leave the pale inner leaves whole. Cover and place in the refrigerator until ready for use.

3 To make the dressing, place the anchovy fillets in base of the salad bowl and mash with the back of a fork while the oil is being added. Gradually add the lemon juice while beating, and sprinkle in the salt and pepper. Break in the coddled egg, scraping the set white from inside the shell and lightly stir. Add the mustard and Worcestershire sauce.

4 Add the lettuce leaves and toss to coat lightly with the dressing while sprinkling over the grated Parmesan cheese. Toss in the chicken and croutons. Rearrange the whole leaves to stand upright and garnish with the shaved Parmesan cheese. Serve immediately.

Serves 5

Marinated Chicken and Pear Salad

Ingredients

I large ready cooked chicken

7oz/200g packet dried pears

Marinade:

½ cup olive oil

½ cup orange juice

2 tbsp red wine vinegar

3 whole cloves

3 small bay leaves

2 tbsp pine nuts

¼ cup raisins

I tsp sweet chili sauce

Salad

I lb/455 g mixed salad greens, crisped

2 Lebanese cucumbers, thinly sliced

I small red onion, sliced

Method

I Remove the flesh from the chicken. Carve the chicken and discard the bones. Place in a flat, non-metal dish and place the dried pears on top.

2 Mix the marinade ingredients together, pour over the chicken and pears, and refrigerate for 2 hours.

3 Place the salad greens on a serving plate, and arrange the chicken strips and pear halves on the salad. Whisk the remaining marinade with a little extra oil and spoon over the salad.

Serves 6–8

Spinach and Almond Chicken Salad

Ingredients

**5 oz/145 g white mushrooms,
   wiped over and sliced**

**14 oz/400 g baby spinach leaves,
   washed and dried**

6 scallions, sliced

2 chicken breast fillets, poached

3 oz/85 g slivered almonds, toasted

crusty bread to serve

Dressing

½ cup olive oil

2 tbsp lemon juice

1 tbsp white wine vinegar

1 clove garlic, crushed

2 tsp Dijon mustard

½ tsp brown sugar

salt and pepper to taste

⅛ tsp nutmeg

Method

1 Mix together the prepared mushrooms, spinach leaves, and scallions. Slice the chicken into long strips and toss with the vegetables.

2 Whisk all the dressing ingredients together and pour over the salad. Add ½ the almonds and toss through. Scatter the remaining almonds over the top of the salad. Serve immediately with crusty bread.

Serves 4

Tossed Greens and Chicken with Blue Cheese Dressing

Ingredients

I bunch arugula

I coral lettuce

I mignonette lettuce

I red apple, cored, thinly sliced, splashed with lemon juice

$1/4$ cup pale walnut pieces

2 poached chicken breasts

Dressing

$1/3$ cup olive oil

2 tbsp white wine vinegar

I tbsp lemon juice

$1/4$ tsp sugar

I tablespoon Dijon mustard

I oz/30 g blue-vein cheese, crumbled

pinch cayenne

2 oz/55 g extra blue-vein cheese for topping

Method

1 Wash the greens, drain, and shake in a kitchen towel to dry. Arrange on 4 individual plates with the apple slices and $1/2$ of the walnuts.

2 Cut the chicken into slices and arrange with the salad greens. Whisk the dressing ingredients together and pour over each salad. Sprinkle top with the remaining walnuts and the extra crumbled blue-vein cheese. Serve as an entrée or for lunch.

Serves 4-5

Italian Chicken in a Pan

Ingredients

6 chicken breast fillets

seasoned flour

1 egg, beaten

dried breadcrumbs

4 tbsp vegetable oil

1 lb /455 g jar tomato pasta sauce

6 slices prosciutto or ham

6 slices mozzarella cheese

6 sprigs fresh sage

Method

1 Place the chicken between sheets of waxed paper and pound lightly to flatten. Dust with the flour, then dip in the egg, and finally coat with the breadcrumbs. Place on a plate lined with plastic wrap, cover, and refrigerate for 15 minutes.

2 Heat the oil in a large frying pan over a medium heat. Add the chicken and cook for 2–3 minutes on each side or until golden. Remove from the pan and set aside. Pour off the oil and wipe the pan with kitchen paper. Add the pasta sauce to the pan, stirring over a medium heat until hot.

3 Place the chicken in a single layer on top of the sauce, then top each fillet with a slice of prosciutto or ham, a slice of cheese and a sprig of sage. Cover and simmer for 5 minutes or until the chicken is cooked through and the cheese melts. Serve immediately.

Serves 6

Warm Salad of Mustard-Glazed Chicken with Red Wine Vinaigrette

Ingredients

3 tbsp mustard seeds

3 tbsp malt vinegar

2 tbsp honey

1 tbsp molasses

1 tbsp brown sugar

1/2 cup olive oil

4 tbsp French mustard

2 cloves garlic, ground

1/2 cup boiling water

8 skinless chicken breast fillets

2 tbsp red or white wine vinegar

2 tbsp olive oil

salt and pepper to taste

10 oz/285 g assorted baby lettuce leaves, well washed and dried

10 oz/285 g baby spinach leaves, well washed and dried

1 bunch scallions, sliced on the diagonal

1 bunch chives, chopped

sprinkle of sesame seeds to garnish

Method

1 To make the marinade, grind 2 tablespoons of the mustard seeds into A powder, then mix with the malt vinegar, honey, molasses, brown sugar, olive oil, French mustard, garlic, and boiling water. Whisk well until the mixture is thick and smooth.

2 Reserve 4 tablespoons of the marinade for later use. Lay the chicken in a flat glass dish and pour the remaining marinade over. Turn the chicken so that both sides are covered in the marinade and chill for at least 4 hours.

3 Remove the chicken from the marinade, making sure that each piece of chicken has a good coating of the marinade. Place in an ovenproof baking dish or on an oven tray and bake at 410°F/210°C/Gas Mark 6 for 20–25 minutes, until cooked through.

4 Meanwhile, transfer the reserved marinade to a saucepan and bring to the boil. Simmer for 5 minutes, then remove from the heat. Remove the chicken from the oven and keep warm.

5 Make a dressing with the red or white wine vinegar and olive oil with salt and pepper to taste and a little of the reserved warm marinade. Whisk well. Toss some dressing through the mixed lettuce and spinach leaves just to coat them. Add the scallions and chives and toss again.

6 To serve, arrange the salad leaves on plates, then top each mound of salad with a chicken breast, sliced on the diagonal. Drizzle around a little remaining warm marinade.

Serves 8

Tropical Chicken Salad

Ingredients

2 large skinless chicken breast fillets

1 Lebanese cucumber, diced

1 cup diced fresh or unsweetened canned pineapple

1/2 cup diced pawpaw

1/4 cup unsalted cashews

2 green onions, sliced diagonally

2 tbsp chopped fresh cilantro

2 tbsp chopped fresh mint

Chili and Lime Dressing

1 fresh red chili, thinly sliced

finely grated zest of 1 lime

juice of 2 limes

1 tbsp fish sauce

1 tbsp rice wine vinegar

1/2 tsp sesame oil

Method

1 Preheat the barbecue to a high heat.

2 Cook the chicken on the barbecue grill for 4–5 minutes each side or until cooked through. Alternatively, place the chicken in a frying pan and pour water or a mixture of water and wine to cover it. Cover. Bring to simmering. Poach for 10 minutes or until the chicken is cooked. Cool. Cut into thin strips.

3 Place the chicken, cucumber, pineapple, pawpaw, cashews, green onions, cilantro, and mint in a bowl. Toss to combine.

4 To make the Chili and Lime Dressing, place the chili, lime zest and juice, fish sauce, vinegar, and oil in a screwtop jar. Shake to combine. Drizzle the dressing over the salad. Toss. Cover. Refrigerate for at least 15 minutes before serving as this allows the flavors to develop.

Note: If you're in a hurry, buy a cooked chicken from a store that does not smother the bird in fat before or during cooking.

Serves 4

Like poultry, pork is delicious roasted, but it is also great used in stir-fries, kebabs, and pasta. It goes beautifully with chili, prunes, scallions, garlic, parsley, apples and peppercorns. In this section, you will find a wide variety of dishes that will spice up your entertaining.

Pork

Pork Appetizers

Air-Dried Prosciutto Roll–Ups

Ingredients

16 thin prosciutto slices

16 pieces cantaloupe melon

16 pieces creamy blue cheese

16 pitted prunes

toothpicks

Method

1 When required, cut the prosciutto slices in ¹/₂ lengthways.

2 Neatly roll the cantaloupe with the prosciutto and skewer with the toothpicks.

3 Roll the soft blue cheese and prunes with the prosciutto.

Note: Season the blue cheese with walnuts. Replace the cantaloupe with fresh figs. Roll the prosciutto with marinated bocconcini and tomato. Replace the prosciutto with thin sliced of glazed ham.

Serves 8 as an appetizer

Bacon, Shrimp, and Vegetable Kebabs with Dill Dressing

Ingredients

Shrimp Kebabs

4 strips of bacon

12 green jumbo shrimps

4 bamboo skewers, soaked in water

lemon wedges to serve

Vegetable Kebabs

4 strips bacon

1 large zucchini, thickly sliced

1 small red bell pepper,
  cut into 3/4 in/2 cm cubes

1 small green bell pepper,
  cut into 3/4 in/2 cm cubes

8 baby yellow squash

8 cherry tomatoes

1 small red onion,
  cut into 1/8

Dressing

2 tbsp oil

2 tbsp lemon juice

1 tbsp teriyaki sauce

1 1/2 tbsp chopped dill

2 cloves garlic, crushed

2 tsp grated fresh ginger

2 tsp sweet chili sauce

Method

1 To make the Shrimp Kebabs, remove the rind from the bacon, and cut crossways into 3 pieces. Peel the shrimps, leaving the tail intact, and remove the back vein. Thread the bacon and shrimps alternately onto 4 skewers.

2 To make Vegetable Kebabs, remove the rind from the bacon. Cut the strips crossways into 3, and roll each piece. Thread the bacon rolls, zucchini, red and green pepper, squash, tomatoes, and onion alternately onto 4 skewers.

3 Combine all the dressing ingredients in a small bowl.

4 Cook the kebabs on the barbecue for 4 minutes on each side or until the bacon is crisp and lightly golden and the vegetables are tender. Brush occasionally with the dressing during cooking. Serve the Shrimp Kebabs with the lemon wedges.

Note: Kebabs can also be broiled for about 3 minutes on each side or until lightly golden.

Serves 4

Chili Pork Tortillas

Ingredients

1 lb/455 g pork stirfry

salt and pepper

8 medium soft flour tortillas

16 large green lettuce leaves

**fresh tomato salsa with avocado,
cilantro and lime juice**

reduced–fat sour cream

Spice Rub

2 tbsp vegetable oil

3 garlic cloves, crushed

1 tsp Tabasco sauce to taste

1 tsp dry oregano

**¹/₂ tsp ground allspice or cumin
  to taste**

Method

1 Mix together the Spice Rub ingredients. Combine the pork with the rub, and set aside for 15 minutes or longer.

2 Season the pork with salt and pepper.

3 Heat a nonstick drying pan, wok or barbecue hotplate until medium to hot. Panfry the pork in 1–2 batches for about 1 minute until medium done. Avoid overcooking.

4 Serve the pork on the warm tortillas with the lettuce, tomato salsa with avocado, and cilantro, and a dollop of the sour cream. Roll up each tortilla.

Note: For an extra twist, sprinkle with chili or grated cheese. Toss the lettuce or salad with some salad dressing. Tabasco and chili are optional.

Serves 4

Cold Roast Pork Platter

Ingredients

2¼–4½ lb/1–2 kg/pork roast, loin, scotch, or blade, boneless and rind off
vegetable oil
1 tsp roast meat seasoning
2 garlic cloves, ground

Method

1 Preheat the oven to 440°F/220°C/Gas Mark 7.

2 Rub the pork with the oil, seasoning, and garlic and place on a rack in an oven dish and roast for 20 minutes until it starts to brown.

3 Reduce the heat to 350°F/170–180°C/Gas Mark 4 and cook until medium done. Allow about 25–30 minutes per 1 lb/455 g for the remainder of the cooking. Pork is cooked when the juices of the meat run clear while pierced in the thickest part with a clean fork or skewer. Ideally, use a meat thermometer to check the temperature away from the bone. The roast is cooked when the internal temperature is 200°F/71°C.

4 Allow the pork to rest for 10–15 minutes. Place the roast on a clean dish, cover, and chill quickly in the coldest part of the refrigerator. Slice when cold and present with antipasto vegetables and salads.

Serves 4–8

Cumin Spiced Pork Kebabs

Ingredients

1 tbsp ground cumin

¹/₄ tsp cayenne pepper

1 tsp dried parsley flakes

1 tsp dried oregano flakes

1 lb/455g lean diced pork pieces
   (³/₄x³/₄ in/2cmx2cm cubes)

2 tbsp olive oil

8 skewers soaked in water for
   1–2 hours

Method

1 Combine the cumin, cayenne, parsley, and oregano. Rub the spices evenly into the pork and thread onto the skewers.

2 Lightly brush the skewers with the oil before and during cooking. Cook on a lightly oiled barbecue or grill on medium-high heat for 5–6 minutes (turn 2–3 times) or until the juices run just pink to clear when pierced with a skewer.

3 Allow the pork to rest for a few minutes before serving.

4 Serve with almond, apricot and cilantro couscous.

Serves 4

Pork Mains

Butterfly Pork with Sweet and Sour Vegetables

Ingredients

4 lean pork butterfly steaks
  (approximately ¼ in/1 cm thick)
2 green onions, thinly sliced
1 in/3 cm piece ginger, peeled
  and grated
toothpicks
1 tbsp vegetable oil
18 oz/510 g jar Chinese sweet
  and sour vegetables in sauce
steamed bok choy and rice to serve

Method

1 Place the pork onto a board and spread the green onion and ginger evenly onto 1 side of each butterfly. Fold in ½ and secure with a toothpick.

2 Heat the oil in a large non stick frying pan over a medium-high heat and cook the pork for 2 minutes on each side.

3 Add the sweet and sour vegetables to frying pan and spoon over the pork, allowing to cook a further 3–4 minutes. Turn occasionally. Remove the toothpicks.

4 Serve immediately with steamed bok choy and rice.

Serves 4

Diced Pork with Vegetable Noodles

Ingredients

1 lb/455 g lean diced pork

1 cup chopped leek

2 tbsp olive oil

2 tbsp light soy sauce

1/2 cup sliced celery

1/2 cup broccoli pieces

1/2 cup Chinese noodles, cooked

Method

1 Cut the pork pieces in half. Heat the oil in a wok or frying pan and sauté the leek and pork until lightly browned.

2 Add the soy sauce, reduce the heat, and simmer for 10 minutes. Add the celery and broccoli, cook a further 2 minutes, then stir through the cooked noodles. Serve immediately.

Serves 4

Italian Pork Pasta

Ingredients

1 1/2 lb/680 g pork schnitzels or
   pork leg steaks, cut into strips
1 small eggplant, quartered
   and thinly sliced
1 tsp olive oil
1 leek, thinly sliced
2 cloves garlic, chopped
1–2 tsp chili sauce
2 tbsp low-salt tomato paste and
   2 tbsp water, combined
6 rashes bacon, chopped
3 oz/85 g mushrooms/ sliced
1 tbsp fresh chopped basil
8 oz/225 g fettuccini pasta
salt and freshly ground black
pepper

Method

1 Cut the pork into thin strips.

2 Sprinkle the eggplant with the salt, let stand for 1 hour, rinse, and pat dry. Lightly pan fry, and remove.

3 To the pan add the oil and lightly sauté the leek and garlic. Add the chili sauce, combined tomato paste, and tomatoes, and cook 2–3 minutes. Add the bacon, mushrooms, and basil.

4 Cook the pasta until al dente in boiling water, then drain.

5 In a nonstick frying pan, lightly panfry pork in 2–3 batches, cooking for 2–3 minutes. Add to the vegetable sauce.

6 Fold the pasta through the pork and sauce, and season with salt and freshly ground black pepper. Serve immediately.

Serves 4–6

Moroccan Spiced Pork

Ingredients

1 lb/455g lean pork stirfry strips

2¹/₂ tsp ground cilantro

1¹/₂ tsp ground cumin

1 tsp ground sweet paprika

1 tsp chili paste

2¹/₂ tbsp vegetable oil

2 cloves garlic, cut into slices

1¹/₂ tsp grated fresh ginger

9 oz/255 g pumpkin, cut into thin
   pieces or slices

3¹/₂ oz/100 g baby English spinach
   leaves

2 tbsp freshly chopped cilantro

1 tbsp fresh lemon juice

couscous to serve

Method

1   Combine the ground cilantro, cumin, paprika, and chili paste. Rub into the pork.

2   Use 2 tablespoons of the oil to cook the pork. Heat ¹/₂ the oil in a large wok over a medium-high heat, add ¹/₂ the pork and stirfry for 1–2 minutes, stirring continuously. Transfer to a plate and cover loosely with foil and set aside. Repeat with the remaining pork.

3   Reduce the heat to medium, add the remaining oil, and cook the garlic for 2 minutes. Add the ginger and pumpkin and cook for 3 minutes, stirring continuously.

4   Return the pork to the wok, add the spinach, cilantro, and lemon juice. Stir to combine and cook for 2 minutes to heat the pork through. Serve immediately with couscous.

Serves 4

Cashew Pork Stirfry

Ingredients

1 lb/455 g pork stirfry strips

2 tbsp peanut oil

2¹/₂ oz/75 g roasted cashew nuts

2 cloves garlic, crushed

1 onion, diced

¹/₂ each green, red, and yellow bell peppers, diced

10 snowpeas, halved

Sauce

2 tbsp fish sauce to taste

2 tbsp oyster sauce

¹/₂ tbsp brown sugar to taste

2 tsp cornstarch

¹/₂ cup salt-reduced chicken bouillon

Method

1 Mix all the sauce ingredients together. Stirfry the cashew nuts until golden and set aside.

2 Slice the pork and vegetables into even, thin strips or cut into even bit-sized pieces.

3 Heat a wok or non stick frying pan until hot. Drizzle in the oil and swirl to lightly glaze and coat the bottom and sides. Stir fry the garlic for about 15 seconds until fragrant. Stirfry the pork in 1–2 batches until just cooked. Allow the pan to reheat between the batches. Remove from the pan.

4 Add a little more hot oil to the wok, and stirfry the harder vegtables first for about 30 seconds to 1 minute or until bright, hot but still crisp. Save softer, leafy and easy to wilt vegetables to the end

5 Return the pork to the hot wok, and lightly combine with vegetables.

6 Make a well by pushing the pork and vegtables to the side. Pour the sauce into the pan and stir to the simmer, tossing the pork meat and vegetables through the sauce whilst heating. Garnish with the cashew nuts and serve immediately.

Serves 4

Peppercorn Pork Chops

Ingredients

4–8 pork chops or steaks

2 tbsp olive oil

ground rock salt and mixed peppercorns

gravy, apple sauce

Vegetable Gratin

4 medium potatoes, peeled

2 carrots, peeled

2 parsnips, peeled

1 oz/30 g butter to taste

1 cup milk, approximately

1/4 cup grated Parmesan or cheese

Method

1 To make the Vegetable Gratin, dice all the vegetables and wash. Cook together in lightly salted water until tender. Drain mash, and mix through the butter and milk. Taste and adjust accordingly. Place the vegetable mash into an oven dish. Sprinkle with the Parmesan and bake until golden brown and hot.

2 Trim the pork, brush with the olive oil, and season with freshly ground salt and peppercorns.

3 Heat a nonstick pan or barbecue until hot. Cook the pork chops to medium done. Rest for 3 minutes in a warm place.

4 Serve with the Vegetable Gratin, gravy, and apple sauce.

Note: Season the Vegetable Gratin with nutmeg and chopped parsley.

Serves 4

Stuffed Pork Scotch

Ingredients

3 1/3 lb/1 1/2 kg pork scotch or pork neck ask your butcher to cut pocket for stuffing
3 tsp five spice powder
1 tsp sea salt, plus extra sea salt
freshly ground black pepper
4 cloves garlic, crushed
zest of 1 large orange

Stuffing
4 scallions, finely sliced
1/2 oz/15g butter
1/2 cup cooked jasmine rice
1/3 cup pineapple pieces, drained
1/4 cup toasted pecan nuts, chopped
salt and pepper

Method

1 Combine the five spice powder, sea salt, and pepper, and rub evenly all over the pork. Rub in the garlic and orange zest. Cover and refrigerate for 2 hours.

2 To make the stuffing, saute the scallions until soft in the butter. Add the rice, and pineapple pieces. Mix to combine. Remove from the heat and stir through the pecan nuts. Season to taste.

3 Place the stuffing in the pocket and tie securely at 2 in/5 cm intervals with twine.

4 Score the pork rind and lay it over the opening. Spray with olive oil and rub with the extra salt. Tie the crackling securely on to the meat (this will prevent it from curling up).

5 Roast at 440°F/220°C/Gas Mark 7 for 20 minutes. Turn down the heat to 350°F/180°C/Gas Mark 4 and roast for another 1 1/4 hours. Remove and leave to stand in a warm place for 10 minutes. Cut off strings before slicing and serving.

Serves 6–8

Roast Pork with Capers and Lemon

Ingredients

3 1/3 lb/1 1/2 kg boned pork loin,
   with rind scored

1 tbsp rinsed capers, finely chopped

1 tsp grated lemon rind

1 tbsp fresh lemon thyme leaves

2 tbsp finely chopped fresh parsley

2 tbsp olive oil

1 lemon, juiced

sea salt

Method

1 Preheat the oven to 440°F/220°C/Gas Mark 7. Combine the capers, lemon rind, thyme, parsley, and 1 tablespoon of oil. Rub the seasoning into the flesh or pork. Roll up the pork and tie to secure with cotton string.

2. Rub the pork rind with the remaining oil, lemon juice and salt ensuring to rub the salt well into the scores (cuts) within the rind. Elevate the pork on a rack in a baking dish.

3 Place the pork into a preheated oven, and cook for 20 minutes. Reduce the heat to 350°F/180°C/Gas Mark 4 and cook for a further 50-50 minutes per kilo or until internal temperature reaches 150°F/70-75°C.

4 Allow the pork to rest for 10 minutes before serving.

5 Serve with the roasted vegetables of parsnip, potato, pumpkin and steamed green beans.

Serves 6

Brandy Peach Ham

Ingredients

6³/₄ oz-9 lb/3-4 kg half leg or shoulder
   ham, bone in or out

Syrup Glaze

¹/₄ cup peach juice

1 cup brown sugar

3 tbsp peach jam

3 tbsp brandy

good pinch mixed spice and cinnamon

Method

1 Preheat the oven to 400°F/200°C/Gas Mark 6. Place all the Syrup Glaze ingredients into a saucepan and stir to simmering point until the sugar dissolves.

2 Gently peel off the pork rind and discard. Be careful not to tear the fat. If you wish, trim and score the fat with a ¹/₄ in/5 mm deep diamond pattern. Weigh the ham to calculate the cooking time.

3 Place the ham on a rack in an oven dish. Brush with the glaze and bake for 20 minutes until the fat starts to open and color. Reduce the heat to 325°F/160–170°C/Gas Mark 3 and cook until hot through. Allow about 10–15 minutes per 1 lb/455 g for the remainder of the cooking and glazing.

4 Brush with the glaze during cooking the ham is cooked when golden in color and the juices are hot when pierced with a clean fork or skewer. 5 Allow ham to rest for 20 minutes.

6 Place the ham on a clean dish, cover and chill quickly in the coldest part of the refrigerator. Slice when cold and serve with potato salad, mustard, or your favourite sauce.

Serves 8–16

In this section, you will find recipes for beef. lamb, and veal, which can provide tasty and hearty meals for your family and friends. Beef and veal go well with bacon, garlic, wine, mushrooms, and many herbs and spices. Lamb goes well with rosemary, garlic, Parmesan cheese, and almonds.

Meat

Meat Appetizers

Skewered Beef Rollettes

Ingredients

115 g/4 oz ricotta cheese

**1 tbsp each chopped parsley
and basil or chives**

1 tbsp chopped scallions

2 tsp lemon juice

freshly ground pepper

**6–8 slices smoked beef or
pastrami**

8–12 small bamboo skewers

6 scallions, cut into short lengths

24 red or yellow cherry tomatoes

selection of salad greens

Method

1   Combine the ricotta, herbs, scallions, and lemon juice. Season to taste. Spread the cheese mixture on the slices of meat and roll up firmly. Pack into a container, cover, and chill until required.

2   Cut each roll into 2–3 pieces. Thread the rollettes on to the skewers, alternating with lengths of the scallion and tomatoes. Serve on the salad greens with light mayonnaise on the side if desired.

Note: These rollettes may be served with a rice or pasta salad, or arrange them on cocktail sticks and serve with drinks.

Serves 6

Spiced Apricot Meatballs with Apricot Dipping Sauce

Ingredients

Meatballs
3/4 cup dried diced apricots
2 tbsp brandy
I lb/455 g prime ground beef
I medium onion, very finely
  chopped
I slice white bread, crusts removed
  and soaked in 1/4 cup water
1/2 tsp ground cinnamon
pinch of ground nutmeg
I tsp salt
1/2 tsp pepper
I egg
oil for frying

Apricot Dipping Sauce
1/2 cup dried diced apricots
I cup water
2 tsp sugar
2 tsp balsamic vinegar
I tsp teriyaki sauce
I tsp fresh ginger juice

Method

I First, make the meatballs. Soak the diced apricots in the brandy for I hour. In a large bowl, combine the ground beef with the remaining meatball ingredients except the oil. Knead well with your hands for 2 minutes to distribute the ingredients evenly and to make a fine-textured mixture. Cover and refrigerate for I hour to allow the flavours to blend.

2 Take a heaped teaspoon of the mixture and roll it into a ball with wet hands. Flatten slightly and press your thumb in the center to form a deep depression. Place 1/4 teaspoon of the soaked apricots in the centre and remold the ball to cover the apricots. Place on a flat tray and roll the remaining balls. Cover with plastic wrap and refrigerate for at least 30 minutes before frying.

3 Heat enough oil to be 1/2 in/I cm deep in a large, heavy-based frying pan or an electric frying pan set at 350°F/180°C. Fry the meatballs in 2 or 3 batches, rolling them around the pan to cook them all over and to keep their shape. Drain on paper towel. Place on a heated serving platter, with the Apricot Dipping Sauce in the center and toothpicks for serving.

4 To make the Apricot Dipping Sauce, place the diced apricots and water in a saucepan with any remaining brandy-soaked apricots. Bring to the boil, turn down the heat, and simmer for 15 minutes or until very soft. Stir in the sugar, vinegar, and teriyaki sauce and simmer for 2 minutes. Purée in a blender or pass through a sieve. Stir in the fresh ginger juice. Serve with the apricot meatballs.

Makes 20–25

Sausage Puffs

Ingredients

1 sheet frozen puff pastry, thawed

13 oz/370 g ground sausage

4 shallots, finely chopped

1 tbsp chutney

1 tsp curry powder

salt and pepper

Method

1 Cut the pastry sheet in half. Combine the rest of the ingredients and mix well. Divide the mixture into 4 and roll into a sausage shape. Place 1 sausage roll on each piece of pastry. Roll the pastry up, sealing the edges with water. Cut the pastry into ½ in/1cm slices.

2 Place the puffs on a sheet of baking paper on a baking tray and cook in a moderately hot oven for about 15 minutes or until golden. Cut into pieces and serve with toothpicks and dipping sauce of your choice.

Makes 10–12

Carpaccio

Ingredients

1 lb/455 g piece beef eye tenderloin

2 breadsticks

3 oz/85 g butter

2 tbsp grated Parmesan cheese

2 tsp grated lemon rind

1/3 cup tartare sauce

1 tbsp chopped anchovy fillets

2 tbsp chopped capers

parsley to garnish

Method

1 Ask your butcher to cut the tenderloin into paper thin slices.

2 Cut the breadsticks into 1/2 in/1cm slices, place in a single layer on a baking tray and bake in a moderate to slow oven at 325°F/150°C/Gas Mark 3 for 10 minutes or until the bread is crisp but not dry. Cool.

3 Spread thinly with the combined butter, cheese, and lemon rind.

4 Place a slice of beef tenderloin onto each bread slice, top with a little tartare sauce, anchovy, and capers. Garnish with the parsley.

Makes about 60

Curried Lamb
Patty Shells

Ingredients

7 oz/200g lamb eye of loin or fillet, finely chopped

3/4 cup continental Thai peanut curry sauce

2 x 2 oz/55 g packets patty shells

24 sprigs of cilantro or herb of your choice

Method

1 Heat a non stick frying pan over a high heat. Add the lamb and fry for 2 minutes.

2 Add the sauce, and cook, uncovered, for 10 minutes, stirring occasionally. Spoon into the patty shells.

3 Preheat the oven to 350°F/180°C/Gas Mark 4. Cook for 10 minutes. Serve hot, garnished with sprigs of cilantro or a herb of your choice.

Makes 24

Cocktail Meatballs

Ingredients

9 oz/255 g ground beef

1 onion, grated

2 tbsp dried breadcrumbs

1/2 tsp salt

1 egg

1 tbsp chopped parsley

1/4 tsp pepper

1/4 tsp oregano

1 teaspoon Tabasco sauce

a little Worcestershire sauce

tomato ketchup

Filling

8 dried prunes, pitted and chopped

1 tbsp pine nuts, coarsely chopped

Method

1 Mix the ground beef and all the ingredients except the Worcestershire sauce for the meatballs together. Knead well with your hands until the beef becomes fine in grain. Allow to stand for 15 minutes before rolling.

2 Combine the prunes and pine nuts. Wet the palms of your hands to prevent the beef sticking, and take about a tablespoon of beef. Roll it into a ball, then flatten in the palm of your hand.

3 Place 1/2 teaspoon of the filling in the center and remold into a smooth ball. Space around the edge of a large dinner plate, and glaze the meatballs with the Worcestershire sauce.

4 Cook the meatballs in the microwave on high for 5 minutes. Cover with the foil and stand for 1 1/2 minutes.

5 Serve with a spicy plum dipping sauce.

Note: Dried apricots or raisins may be used instead of prunes and walnuts, and almonds in place of pine nuts. You can also make the meatballs without the stuffing, but cook 4 minutes only. Serve with tomato ketchup.

Makes 16 small meatballs

Mini Beef Satays

Ingredients

1²/₃ oz/750 g lean round, boneless blade
   or topside steak

24 cocktail bamboo skewers

¹/₄ cup white wine

2 tsp soy sauce

2 tsp satay sauce

¹/₄ tsp chili sauce

1 clove garlic, crushed

1 tbsp soft brown sugar

strips of chili to garnish

Method

1 Soak the cocktail bamboo skewers for 30 minutes to prevent burning. Slice the meat thinly and evenly into 3 in/8 cm strips. Weave the strips onto the skewers.

2 Combine the wine, sauces, garlic, and brown sugar and place in a glass or ceramic dish. Add the satays, turning them in the mixture to coat. Leave to marinate in the mixture for at least 30 minutes, turning occasionally.

3 Remove the grill pan and heat the grill on high. Place the satays on the cold grill (to prevent them sticking during cooking) and cook under the grill for 4–5 minutes on each side, basting occasionally with the remaining marinade. Garnish with the chili strips. Serve with peanut sauce if desired.

Makes 24

Salami Stacks

Ingredients

9 oz/255 g cream cheese

3 oz/85 g diced dried apricots

4 tbsp mayonnaise

¹/₂ tsp tabasco sauce

16 slices Danish salami

extra 5 oz/145 g diced apricots,
  very finely chopped

24 toothpicks

Method

1 Bring the cream cheese to room temperature, and cream well, using a wooden spoon, to soften. Reserve 3 tablespoons of the cream cheese, and leave at room temperature. Stir the 3 oz/85 g diced apricots, mayonnaise, and tabasco into the cream cheese.

2 Lay 4 salami slices on a clean board. Spread a heaped teaspoon of the cheese mixture on each slice, making sure it is spread right to the edge. Place the second salami slice on top and spread as above. Repeat with 1 more slice and top with the fourth slice. Place on a flat plate, cover with plastic wrap, and refrigerate for 2 hours.

3 Take the extra 5 oz/145 g of very finely chopped apricots. Spread on paper towel in a ¹/₂ in/1 ¹/₂ cm wide strip. Lightly spread the reserved cream cheese around the sides of the salami stacks. Roll the sides of the stacks over the chopped apricots, pressing on well. Cover and refrigerate. To serve, cut each stack into 6 triangles. Place a toothpick in the center of each and arrange on a platter.

Makes 24

Olive Biscuits with Thyme-Cured Beef

Ingredients

chutney of your choice

fresh thyme sprigs

Thyme-Cured Beef

6 oz/170 g sugar

4 oz/115 g salt

3 tbsp crushed black peppercorns

1 large bunch (about 2 oz/55 g) fresh thyme, leaves only

7 oz/200 g lean beef fillet, trimmed of visible fat

Olive Biscuits

oil for greasing

9 oz/255 g all-purpose flour

2 tsp baking powder

1½ oz/45 g black olives, chopped

1 tbsp chopped fresh basil

freshly ground black pepper

1 cup buttermilk

1 tbsp Dijon mustard

Method

1 To cure the beef, place the sugar, salt, peppercorns, and thyme leaves on a large plate. Roll the beef in the mixture several times to coat and form a crust. Place the beef on a wire rack set in a shallow dish. Cover and refrigerate for 24 hours, checking occasionally that the crust remains intact.

2 Using absorbent paper towel, thoroughly wipe away the herb crust. Using a sharp knife, cut the beef across the grain into paper-thin slices – this is easier if you place the fillet in the freezer for 10 minutes before slicing. Place the slices on a plate, cover, and refrigerate until ready to use.

3 To make the Olive Biscuits, preheat the oven to 400°F/200°C/Gas Mark 6. Lightly brush a baking tray with the oil and set aside.

4 Into a large bowl, sift the flour and baking powder. Add the olives, basil, and black pepper to taste. Mix to combine. Make a well in the center. In a small bowl, place the milk and mustard. Whisk to combine and pour into the flour mixture. Mix quickly to make a soft dough. Turn the dough onto a lightly floured surface. Knead lightly until smooth.

5 Press the dough or roll out to form a ³/₄ in/2 cm thick rectangle. Using a 1 in/3 cm biscuit cutter, cut out the biscuits. Place with the sides just touching on the prepared baking tray. Bake for 10–12 minutes or until the biscuits are well risen and golden. Transfer to a wire rack. Cool slightly.

6 To serve, split the biscuits and spread with a little relish.. Top with a small mound of beef and a thyme sprig.

Makes 24 biscuits or 48 open-faced canapés

Meat Mains

Steak and Kidney Pie

Ingredients

2¼ lb/1 kg lean topside steak,
  cut into 1 in/2½ cm cubes

6 lamb's kidneys or 1 ox kidney,
  cored and roughly chopped

4 tbsp flour

1 tbsp vegetable oil

2 cloves garlic, crushed

2 onions, chopped

½ tsp dry mustard

2 tbsp chopped fresh parsley

2 tbsp Worcestershire sauce

1½ cup beef bouillon

2 tsp tomato paste

12 oz/340 g prepared puff pastry

2 tbsp milk

Method

1 Place the steak, kidneys, and flour in a plastic food bag and shake to coat the meat with the flour. Shake off the excess flour and set aside. Heat the oil in a large frying pan and cook the meat over a high heat, stirring, until brown on all sides. Reduce the heat to medium, add the garlic and onions, and cook for 3 minutes longer.

2 Stir in the mustard, parsley, Worcestershire sauce, bouillon, and tomato paste, bring to simmering point, cover, and simmer, stirring occasionally, for 2½ hours or until the meat is tender. Remove the pan from the heat and set aside to cool completely.

3 Place the cooled filling in a 4 cup capacity pie dish. On a lightly floured surface, roll out the pastry to 2 in/5 cm larger than the pie dish. Cut off a ½ in/1 cm strip from the pastry edge. Brush the rim of the dish with water and press the pastry strip onto the rim. Brush the pastry strip with water. Lift the pastry top over the filling and press gently to seal the edges. Trim and knock back the edges to make a decorative edge. Brush with the milk and bake at 420°F/210°C/Gas Mark 7 for 30 minutes or until the pastry is golden and crisp.

Serves 6

Sausage and Pancetta Risotto

Ingredients

2 tbsp olive oil

3 oz/85 g pancetta or rindless back bacon, chopped

1 small carrot, sliced

1 onion, thinly sliced

2 x 14 oz/400 g cans chopped tomatoes

2$^{1}/_{4}$ cups chicken bouillon

6 oz/170 g drained canned kidney beans

1 oz/30 g butter

4 Italian sausages, casings removed

$^{1}/_{2}$ tsp dried sage

$^{1}/_{2}$ tsp dried rosemary

2 cloves garlic, crushed

6 oz/170 g arborio rice

$^{1}/_{2}$ cup red wine

$^{1}/_{2}$ red or yellow bell pepper, roughly chopped

3 oz/85 g grated Parmesan cheese

Method

1 Heat the oil in a large frying pan, add the pancetta or bacon, carrot, and onion and fry for 10 minutes, stirring occasionally. Stir in the tomatoes, lower the heat and simmer for 15 minutes. Stir in the bouillon and beans, remove the pan from heat, and set aside.

2 In a saucepan, melt the butter and fry the sausages with the sage, rosemary, and garlic for 7 minutes, stirring frequently until the sausage is crumbly.

3 Add the rice and wine. Stir the mixture until the liquid has evaporated, then add 1 cup of the bean bouillon mixture. Cook until the liquid has evaporated.

4 Continue adding the bean bouillon mixture in this fashion until all the liquid has been absorbed and the rice is tender, about 20 minutes. Stir in the chopped bell pepper and Parmesan and serve immediately.

Serves 4

Veal Scallops

Ingredients

8 small, thin veal steaks

seasoned flour

1 egg, lightly beaten

6 oz/170 g breadcrumbs, made
from stale bread

2oz/55g butter

8 slices prosciutto

4 oz/115 g grated mozzarella cheese

3 tbsp grated fresh Parmesan cheese

½ cup heavy thickened cream
(double)

Method

1   Place the veal slices between plastic wrap and flatten, using a mallet, until very thin. Coat the veal in the flour, dip in the egg, then coat with the breadcrumbs.

2   Melt the butter in a frying pan until foaming. Add the veal and cook for 2 minutes on each side or until golden.

3   Wrap each veal steak in a slice of prosciutto, place in a shallow baking dish, and sprinkle with the mozzarella and Parmesan cheeses. Spoon the cream over and broil for 3–4 minutes, or until the cheese melts and is golden.

Note: Serve this easy veal dish with a fresh green salad.

Serves 4

Lamb Pot Roast

Ingredients

3 oz/85 g butter

3–4 lb/1½–2 kg leg of lamb

14 oz/400 g canned tomatoes, mashed and undrained

½ cup red wine

2 tbsp tomato paste

1 tbsp Worcestershire sauce

½ tsp mixed dried herbs

1 tsp sugar

freshly ground black pepper

olive oil

3 carrots, peeled and halved lengthwise

3 turnips, peeled and halved lengthwise

6 small onions, peeled

3 large potatoes, peeled and halved

Method

1 Melt 1 oz/30 g of the butter in a large heavy-based saucepan and cook the meat on all sides until well browned.

2 Combine the tomatoes, red wine, tomato paste, Worcestershire sauce, herbs, sugar, and black pepper to taste. Pour over the meat, bring to the boil, then reduce heat, cover, and simmer for 1½ hours or until the meat is tender.

3 About 30 minutes before the meat finishes cooking, heat the oil and remaining butter in a large heavy-based frying pan. Add the carrots, turnips, onions, and potatoes and cook until the vegetables are lightly browned. Reduce the heat to low and cook gently for 15–20 minutes or until the vegetables are tender.

4 Remove the meat from the pan, place on a serving platter, and set aside to keep warm. Bring the sauce that remains in the pan to the boil and cook for 10 minutes or until the sauce reduces and thickens slightly. Serve the sauce with the meat and vegetables.

Note: A nut of veal, a whole chicken, or a piece of topside beef are also delicious cooked in this way. Pot roasting dates back to prehistoric times when clay pots were filled with game, whole cuts of meat or poultry and vegetables, then hung over a fire to simmer. Lean meats that need long slow cooking are ideal for pot roasting.

Serves 6

Almond Lamb Pilau

Ingredients

2 tbsp olive oil

1 onion, chopped

1 clove garlic, crushed

1 lb/455 g diced lamb

2 tsp curry powder

2 tsp ground cilantro

1 tsp ground cumin

1 tsp ground ginger

$\frac{1}{2}$ teaspoon ground turmeric

2$\frac{1}{2}$ cups chicken bouillon

1 tomato, chopped

freshly ground black pepper

2 cups rice

3 oz/85 g almonds, toasted

3 oz/85 g raisins

Method

1 Heat the oil in a frying pan over a medium heat, add the onion and garlic and cook, stirring, for 5 minutes or until the onion is tender. Add the lamb and cook, stirring occasionally, for 5 minutes or until the lamb is brown on all sides.

2 Add the curry powder, cilantro, cumin, ginger, and turmeric to the pan and cook, stirring constantly, for 2 minutes or until fragrant. Add $\frac{1}{2}$ cup bouillon, tomato, and black pepper to taste and bring to the boil. Reduce the heat, cover, and simmer, stirring occasionally, for 20 minutes or until the lamb is tender.

3 Add the remaining bouillon to the pan and bring to the boil. Stir in the rice, reduce the heat, cover, and simmer for 15 minutes or until the rice is cooked. Add the almonds and raisins and, using a fork, toss to combine.

Serves 6

Sweet Meat Curry

Ingredients

2 tbsp olive oil

I onion, chopped

I clove garlic, crushed

I tbsp curry powder

I tsp ground ginger

I tsp chopped fresh red chili (optional)

2 carrots, chopped

2 stalks celery, chopped

I apple, chopped

I banana, sliced

2 tbsp golden raisins

2 tbsp malt vinegar

I tbsp fruit chutney

2 tsp brown sugar

2¹/₂ cups water

freshly ground black pepper

¹/₄ cup flour blended with ¹/₃ cup water

I lb/455 g chopped cooked beef,
   lamb, pork, or chicken

Method

1 Heat the oil in a large saucepan over a medium heat, add the onion and garlic and cook, stirring, for 3–4 minutes or until the onion is tender. Add the curry powder, ginger, and chili, if using, and cook for 1 minute or until fragrant.

2 Add the carrots, celery, apple, banana, golden raisins, vinegar, chutney, and sugar and cook for 2–3 minutes. Stir in the water and black pepper to taste and bring to the boil. Reduce the heat, cover, and simmer for 15–20 minutes or until the vegetables are tender.

3 Stir the flour mixture into the curry and cook, stirring constantly, for 5 minutes or until the mixture boils and thickens. Stir in the meat and simmer for 5–10 minutes or until heated through.

Note: Serve the curry with rice and traditional Indian accompaniments such as pappadums, relish and sambals, or boiled potatoes and steamed vegetables.

Serves 6

Veal Chops with Sun-Dried Tomatoes

Ingredients

8 veal chops, trimmed of all visible fat

seasoned flour

2 oz/55 g butter

1 clove garlic, crushed

6 slices prosciutto, chopped

2 tbsp chopped fresh rosemary

1 cup dry white wine

16 sun-dried tomatoes, chopped

4 tbsp chopped fresh basil

Method

1 Coat the chops with the flour. Melt the butter in a frying pan and cook the garlic, prosciutto, and rosemary over a high heat for 2 minutes. Add the chops and brown on both sides.

2 Stir in the wine. Bring to the boil, reduce the heat, and simmer for 30 minutes or until the veal is cooked.

3 Remove the chops and prosciutto from the pan and set aside to keep warm. Increase the heat, stir in the tomatoes and cook until the sauce is reduced by half. Stir in the basil and spoon the sauce over the chops and top with the prosciutto.

Note: Sun-dried tomatoes are becoming increasingly popular and are available from most delicatessens.

Serves 4

Daube of Beef

Ingredients

**2¼ lb/1 kg chuck or blade steak,
    trimmed of all visible fat and cubed**
½ cup seasoned flour
¼ cup olive oil
1 onion, chopped
1 clove garlic, crushed
1 leek, sliced
2 cups beef bouillon
1 cup red wine
1 tsp dried mixed herbs
freshly ground black pepper
1 bay leaf
few thin strips orange rind, optional
2 zucchini, sliced
1 large sweet potato, chopped
1 parsnip, sliced

Method

1 Toss the beef in the flour. Shake off the excess and set aside. Heat ½ the oil in a large frying pan over a medium heat, and cook the beef in batches for 3–4 minutes or until brown. Place in a casserole dish.

2 Heat the remaining oil in the same pan, add the onion and garlic, and cook over a medium heat, stirring, for 4–5 minutes. Add the leek and cook for 2–3 minutes longer. Add the vegetables to the casserole dish.

3 Add the bouillon, wine, herbs, and black pepper to taste to the pan and stirring, bring to the boil. Reduce the heat and simmer until the liquid reduces by half. Add the bouillon mixture, bay leaf, and orange rind, if using, to the casserole dish and bake for 1½–2 hours at 420°F/210°C/Gas Mark 7 or until the beef is tender.

4 Add the zucchini, sweet potato, and parsnip, and bake for an extra 30 minutes or until the vegetables are tender.

Serves 4

Beef and Bean Stir-fry

Ingredients

2 tsp vegetable oil

2 cloves garlic, crushed

**1 lb/455 g topside or round steak,
   cut into thin strips**

**6 oz/170 g snake or green beans, cut into
   4 in/10 cm lengths**

2 kaffir lime leaves, shredded

2 tsp brown sugar

2 tbsp light soy sauce

1 tbsp Thai fish sauce

2 tbsp cilantro leaves

Method

1 Heat the oil and garlic together in a wok over a medium heat. Increase the heat to high, and add the beef, and stirfry for 3 minutes or until the beef changes color.

2 Add the beans, lime leaves, sugar, and soy and fish sauces and stirfry for 2 minutes or until the beans change color. Stir in the cilantro and serve immediately.

Note: Kaffir limes are a popular Thai ingredient. Both the fruit and the leaves have a distinctive flavor and perfume and are used in cooking. The leaves are available dried, fresh frozen, or fresh from oriental food shops and some greengrocers. If kaffir lime leaves are unavailable, a little finely grated lime rind can be used instead.

Serves 4

Carpetburgers with Caper Mayonnaise

Ingredients

1 lb/455 g lean ground beef

8 oz/225 g sausage meat

4 scallions, finely chopped

2 cloves garlic, crushed

2 tsp finely grated lemon zest

1 tsp finely chopped fresh dill

18 bottled oysters

3 bacon strips, cut in half lengthwise
    and rind removed

wooden toothpicks or cocktail sticks

2 tbsp red wine

2 tbsp olive oil

Caper Mayonnaise

2 tbsp mayonnaise

$1/2$ cup heavy cream

2 tsp chopped capers

1 tsp finely grated lemon rind

1 small gherkin, finely chopped

Method

1 Place the sbeef, sausage meat, scallions, garlic, lemon rind, and dill in a bowl and mix to combine. Shape the mixture into 12 patties.

2 Top $1/2$ of the patties with 3 oysters each, then, with the remaining patty, pinch the edges together to join and completely seal the filling. Wrap a piece of bacon around each pattie and secure with wooden toothpicks or cocktail sticks.

3 Place the wine and oil in a large shallow glass or ceramic dish and mix to combine. Add the patties and marinate for 10 minutes.

4 Drain the patties and cook on a preheated medium barbecue for 5–7 minutes on each side or until cooked.

5 To make the Caper Mayonnaise, place the mayonnaise, cream, capers, lemon zest, and gherkin in a bowl and mix to combine. Serve with the patties.

Note: This is more economical, but just as tasty variation on that old favorite, Carpetbag Steak. Prunes, dried apricots, or sliced cheese can be used in place of the oysters.

Serves 6

Crunchy Cottage Pie

Ingredients

1 tbsp olive oil

1 onion, finely chopped

1 clove garlic, crushed

4 oz/115 g mushrooms, sliced

2 bacon strips, chopped

1 lb/455 g lean ground beef

3 tbsp tomato sauce

1 1/2 tbsp Worcestershire sauce

1 tsp soy sauce

1 3/4 cups beef bouillon

1/4 tsp dried thyme

2 tbsp chopped fresh parsley

freshly ground black pepper

Crunchy Vegetable Topping

3 large potatoes, chopped

8 oz/225 g pumpkin or carrots, chopped

1 egg, lightly beaten

1/4 cup sour cream

1/4 tsp nutmeg

1/4 cup chopped pumpkin seeds

1/4 cup dried breadcrumbs

1 oz/30 g grated fresh Parmesan cheese

2 oz/55 g butter, melted

Method

1 Heat the oil in a frying pan over a medium heat, add the onion, and cook, stirring, for 1 minute. Add the garlic, mushrooms, and bacon, and cook, stirring constantly, for 2 minutes. Stir in the beef and cook for 5 minutes or until the meat is brown.

2 Stir the tomato sauce, Worcestershire sauce, soy sauce, bouillon, thyme, parsley, and black pepper to taste into the pan. Bring to simmering point and simmer, uncovered, for 25–30 minutes or until the mixture reduces and thickens. Spoon the meat mixture into an ovenproof pie dish.

3 To make the Crunchy Vegetable Topping, place the potatoes, pumpkin or carrots, egg, sour cream, and nutmeg in a bowl and mix to combine. Spoon the vegetable mixture over the meat mixture. Place the pumpkin seeds, breadcrumbs, Parmesan cheese, and butter in a bowl and mix to combine. Sprinkle over the vegetable mixture and bake in a moderate oven 350°F/180°C/Gas Mark 4 for 45 minutes or until the meat mixture is hot and bubbling and the topping is golden.

Note: Any ground meat or combination of ground meats can be used to make this tasty cottage pie. The pie is almost a meal in itself; all you need for a complete meal are steamed green vegetables, such as zucchini, beans, or cabbage.

Serves 4

Lamb and Kidney Loaf

Ingredients

3 lamb kidneys, trimmed of all visible fat

3 bay leaves

6 bacon strips, rind removed

1 oz/30 g butter

1 onion, finely chopped

1/4 cup brandy

1 tbsp finely chopped fresh thyme
or 1 tsp dried thyme

1 tbsp green peppercorns
in brine, drained

1²/₃ lb /750 g lean ground lamb

3/4 cup breadcrumbs, made from
stale bread

1/2 chicken bouillon cube

1 tbsp tomato paste

1 egg, lightly beaten

Green Peppercorn Sauce

2 tbsp brown sugar

1 oz/30 g butter

1/4 cup red wine

2 tbsp brandy

1 cup chicken bouillon

2 tsp green peppercorns
in brine, drained

1/2 cup heavy cream

Method

1 Soak the kidneys in a bowl of salted water for 10 minutes. Drain, then pat dry with absorbent paper towel. Cut into slices, discarding the core, and set aside.

2 Arrange the bay leaves in the base of a greased 4¹/₂ x 8¹/₂ in/11 x 21 cm loaf tin and line the tin with 4 bacon strips.

3 Melt the butter in a frying pan over a medium heat, add the onion and cook for 2–3 minutes or until soft. Add the kidneys and cook for 2–3 minutes or until they just change color. Stir in the brandy, thyme, and green peppercorns and cook, stirring, for 5 minutes or until the brandy reduces by half. Set aside to cool.

4 Place the lamb, breadcrumbs, bouillon cube, tomato paste, egg, and kidney mixture in a bowl and mix to combine. Spoon the lamb mixture into the prepared loaf tin, lay the remaining bacon strips on top, and cover with aluminum foil. Place the tin in a baking dish with enough boiling water to come halfway up the sides of the tin and bake for 45 minutes. Remove the foil, drain off the juices, and bake for 45 minutes longer or until the meatloaf is cooked.

5 To make the Green Peppercorn Sauce, place the sugar and butter in a frying pan and cook over a medium heat, stirring, for 3–4 minutes or until the sugar dissolves. Stir in the wine, brandy, chicken bouillon, and green peppercorns, bring to simmering point, and simmer for 5 minutes or until the sauce reduces and thickens. Whisk in the cream, bring back to simmering, and simmer for 2–3 minutes longer. Serve with the meatloaf.

Serves 8

247

Nasi Goreng

Ingredients

Chili Meatballs

8 oz/225 g lean ground beef

1 onion, finely chopped

1/2 tsp ground red chilli

1/2 tsp curry paste (vindaloo)

1 egg white, lightly beaten

vegetable oil for deep-frying

short bamboo skewers

Nasi Goreng Rice

2 eggs, lightly beaten

1 tbsp soy sauce

1/4 cup groundnut oil

2 onions, thinly sliced

2 cloves garlic, crushed

1/2 red bell pepper, chopped

1/2 green bell pepper, chopped

1 tsp ground red chili

1 boneless chicken breast fillet, chopped

13 oz/370 g fillet pork, chopped

8 oz/225 g uncooked shrimps, shelled and deveined

4 oz/115 g bean sprouts

2 1/4 cups long grain rice, cooked

1 tbsp chopped fresh cilantro

Method

1 To make the Chilli Meatballs, place the beef, onion, chili, curry paste (vindaloo), and egg white in a bowl and mix to combine. Shape the meat mixture into small balls.

2 Heat the vegetable oil in a large saucepan until a cube of bread dropped in browns in 50 seconds. Cook the meatballs a few at a time for 4–5 minutes or until golden and cooked through. Drain the meatballs on absorbent paper towel, then thread onto short bamboo skewers. Set aside and keep warm.

3 For the Nasi Goreng Rice, place the eggs and 1 teaspoon of the soy sauce in a bowl and whisk to combine. Heat 1 tablespoon of the groundnut oil in a heavy-based frying pan over a medium heat, add the egg mixture, and cook, without stirring, until set. Remove the omelette from the pan, cut 1/2 into small pieces and 1/2 into long strips. Set aside.

4 Heat the remaining groundnut oil in the frying pan over a medium heat. Add the onions, garlic, red and green bell peppers and stirfry for 3–4 minutes or until the onion is soft. Add the chili, chicken, and pork and stirfry for 8–10 minutes longer or until the meat is brown.

5 Add the shrimp, bean sprouts, and rice and stir-fry for 4–5 minutes or until the mixture is heated through. Stir in cilantro, chopped omelette, and the remaining soy sauce, and stirfry for 1–2 minutes longer.

6 To serve, spoon the rice into the center of a serving platter, top with the omelette strips, and surround with the skewered meatballs.

Serves 6

Barbecue cooking gives meat, vegetables, or whatever you barbecue, a delicious, smoky flavor unlike any other. You can barbecue anything: pork, lamb, beef, poultry, as well as seafood. Try marinating before you barbecue; the flavor is intensified. Use the recipes in this section to take your entertaining to a new level.

Barbecue

Glazed Pork Spare Ribs

Ingredients

2¼ lb/1 kg pork spare ribs

Soy and Honey Marinade

4 tbsp soy sauce

2 tbsp honey

1 tbsp sherry

2 cloves garlic, crushed

1 tsp grated fresh ginger

Method

1 In a small bowl, combine all the marinade ingredients. Place the spare ribs on a large sheet of heavy-duty foil and cover both sides generously with the marinade. Wrap into a double-folded parcel, making sure all the joins are well sealed to prevent leakage. Stand for at least a ½ hour before cooking.

2 Prepare the barbecue for direct-heat cooking. Place a wire cake-rack on the grill bars to stand 1 in/2½ cm above the bars. Place the ribs in the foil parcel on the rack and cook for 10 minutes on each side.

3 Remove to a plate, remove the ribs from the foil, and discard foil, then return the ribs to rack. Continue cooking for about 10 minutes, brushing with the marinade and turning each minute until the ribs are well browned and crisp.

Serves 4

Barbecued Pork Kebabs

Ingredients

10¹/₂ oz/300 g lean diced pork

1 small onion

1 green bell pepper

4 skewers

Marinade

1¹/₂ tsp salt reduced soy sauce

1 tbsp sherry or wine

1 tsp lemon juice

1 clove garlic, crushed

dash sesame oil

dash chili sauce

Method

1 Combine in a basin the marinade ingredients, add the pork and mix together with a spoon. Stand approximately ¹/₂ hour or covered overnight in the refrigerator.

2 Cut the peeled onion, and bell pepper into wedges and separate pieces.

3 Divide the pork mixture onto 4 skewers or soaked wooden satay sticks. Arrange the pork, onion, and bell peppers alternately onto the skewers.

4 Cook under a preheated griller or barbecue, or on a hot plate, and turn often.

5 Brush over the marinade while cooking, approximately 5 minutes, depending on the size of the diced pork.

6 Serve on a bed of saffron rice and, if desired, with a freshly tossed salad.

Serves 2

Barbecue Pork Wrap

Ingredients

**4 pork leg schnitzels, butterfly,
  or minute steaks**

olive oil

**$1/2$ tbsp barbecue seasoning or sprinkle
  (Cajun, Mexican, or barbecue)**

2 medium onions, sliced

**9 oz/ 255 g arugula or lettuce salad
  with tomato, avocado, crisp bacon
  pieces, cucumber, and scallions**

4 flatbreads, tortillas or lavash

barbecue sauce

Method

1 Cut the pork schnitzels or butterfly steaks in $1/2$. Brush both sides with the olive oil and season with the barbecue seasoning.

2 Heat the barbecue plate or grill bars until hot. Barbecue the onions and keep warm. Cook the pork for about 30 seconds to 1 minute on each side until medium-done and the juices are just pink to clear. Avoid overcooking.

3 Serve the pork on the warm flatbread with the salad, onions, and sauce. Roll and enjoy.

Serves 4

Barbecued Port-Glazed Lamb

Ingredients

5 lb/2¹/₂ kg leg of lamb

1 cup port wine

1¹/₂ cups water

Port Glaze

4 tbsp Dijon mustard

2 tsp finely grated orange rind

¹/₂ tsp grated nutmeg

1¹/₂ cups port wine

¹/₂ cup honey

2 tbsp balsamic vinegar

Method

1 Preheat the covered barbecue to a medium heat.

2 To make the Port Glaze, place the mustard, orange rind, nutmeg, port wine, honey, and vinegar in a saucepan, bring to simmering point over a low heat, and simmer until the mixture thickens and reduces slightly.

3 Place the lamb on a wire rack set in a roasting tin and brush with the glaze. Pour the port wine and water into the roasting tin, cover the barbecue with the lid and cook for 2 hours, brushing with the glaze at 15-minute intervals, or until cooked to your liking.

Serves 8

259

Barbecued Whiting with Sage

Ingredients

14 cup lemon juice

3 tablespoons finely chopped sage

¹/₂ cup olive oil

salt and freshly ground pepper

4 serving size fish such as whiting

sprigs of fresh sage

lemon wedges for garnishing

Method

1 Using a small bowl, whisk the lemon juice and the sage, gradually adding oil in a thin stream. Season with salt and pepper. Wipe the fish well with a kitchen towel and arrange them in a shallow glass or ceramic dish to fit them in one layer. Pour over the marinade. Make sure the fish is well coated with the marinade, cover and leave to marinate for several hours, turning the fish every now and then.

2 Have ready a large sheet of heavy duty foil (you can use a banana leaf the first line the foil). Or use 4 pieces of foil and wrap the fish separately. Make a packet of the fish. Place the packet over glowing coals and cook for 10-15 minutes, turning the packet once. To test if fish is cooked, see if it flakes easily with a fork. Open the packets and transfer the fish carefully with a fish slice to a serving platter or board. Reserve the cooking juices by pouring into a small bowl. Garnish the fish with the fresh sage sprigs and lemon and serve with the reserved juices.

Serves 4

Barbecued Seafood Salad

Ingredients

2 tbsp lemon juice

1 tbsp olive oil

10¹/₂ oz/300 g firm white fish (swordfish, mackerel, or cod cut into 1 in/2¹/₂ cm cubes)

10¹/₂ oz/300 g pink fish (salmon, ocean trout, marlin, or tuna)

12 scallops

12 uncooked shrimps with or without shell

1 calamari, cleaned and tube cut into rings

1 large onion, cut into rings

1 cucumber, sliced thinly

1 bunch watercress, broken into sprigs

Raspberry and Tarragon Dressing

3 tbsp chopped fresh tarragon

2 tbsp raspberry or red wine vinegar

2 tbsp lemon juice

1 tbsp olive oil

freshly ground black pepper

Method

1 Place the lemon juice and oil in a bowl. Whisk to combine. Add the white and pink fish, scallops, shrimps, and calamari. Toss to combine. Cover. Marinate in the refrigerator for 1 hour or until ready to use. Do not marinate for longer than 2 hours.

2 Preheat a barbecue or chargrill pan until very hot. Drain the seafood mixture and place on the barbecue hotplate or in the pan. Add the onion. Cook, turning several times, for 6–8 minutes or until the seafood is just cooked. Take care not to overcook or the seafood will be tough and dry. Transfer the cooked seafood to a bowl and cool, then add the cucumber.

3 Line a serving platter with the watercress, and arrange the seafood and cucumber on top.

4 To make the Raspberry and Tarragon Dressing, place the tarragon, vinegar, lemon juice, oil, and black pepper to taste in a screwtop jar. Shake to combine.

5 Drizzle the dressing over the salad, and serve immediately.

Serves 8

Lamb and Salsa Pockets

Ingredients

½ **leg of lamb, trimmed of fat**

1 tbsp lemon juice

salt and pepper

2 tsp oil

1 clove garlic, crushed

bamboo skewers

6 pitta bread rounds

1 small lettuce, shredded

10 oz/285 g tomato salsa, warmed

Method

1 Preheat the barbecue to a high heat. Soak the bamboo skewers in warm water for 15 minutes. Cut the lamb into ½ in/1 cm cubes. In a large glass bowl, place the lamb, lemon juice, salt, pepper, oil, and garlic. Cover and marinate at room temperature for 20 minutes. Thread onto the skewers.

2 Lightly oil the barbecue plate and cook the lamb skewers for 3–4 minutes on each side. Remove the skewers.

3 Halve the pocket bread and heat a little on the barbecue. Open the pocket, fill with the lettuce, and lamb and top with the heated salsa.

Serves 6

Mini Lamb Roast with Barbecued Noodles

Ingredients

1 trim lamb mini roast
2 tbsp chopped fresh cilantro
1 clove garlic, crushed
salt and pepper
1 tbsp lemon juice
1 tbsp oil

Barbecued Noodles
1 lb/455 g hokkien noodles
1 tbsp chopped fresh cilantro
3¹/₂ oz/100 g feta cheese, crumbled
1 clove garlic, crushed
¹/₂ teaspoon chopped chili, optional

Method

1 Preheat the kettle/weber or hooded gas barbecue for indirect cooking. Tie the mini roast with kitchen string to retain moisture.

2 In a large glass bowl, combine the cilantro, garlic, salt and pepper, lemon juice, and oil. Place the lamb into the marinade and turn to coat on all sides. Marinate for 1 hour at room temperature.

3 Place the lamb over the drip tray in the center of the barbecue, cover with the lid or hood, and cook for 35–40 minutes. There is no need to turn. Alternatively, place the lamb in a foil tray, brushing with the marinade as it cooks. Allow to stand 10–15 minutes before carving.

4 To make the Barbecued Noodles, rinse the noodles in hot water and separate. Drain well. In a small bowl, combine the cilantro, feta, garlic and chili, if using, mixing to a paste.

5 Heat the barbecue plate to high. Lightly oil and add the noodles, tossing with the cilantro paste. Mix well and heat through. (Alternatively, use a baking dish on grill plate to cook the noodles.)

6 Serve the calved lamb on the Barbecued Noodles and drizzle with remaining juices, if desired.

267

This section offers you the opportunity to discover the flavor of vegetables. Use these recipes to tempt your friends and family with something tasty yet different. Vegetables go well with many herbs, spices, oils, and wine. And they can be cooked in an endless variety of ways. Enjoy!

Vegetables

Vegetarian Appetizers

Roman Kebabs

Ingredients

4 wooden skewers

1 French breadstick

14 oz/400 g mozzarella

4 Italian or plum tomatoes

1/3 cup olive oil

1 tbsp lemon juice

1 tsp dried oregano

salt and black pepper

fresh basil to garnish

Method

1 Preheat the oven to 450°F/230°C/Gas Mark 8. Soak 4 wooden skewers in water for 10 minutes.

2 Cut the bread into thick slices, and cut the mozzarella into 12 slices. Slice the tomatoes into 3.

3 Combine the oil, lemon juice, oregano, and seasoning in a shallow dish. Brush both sides of the bread with the oil, thread the bread onto the skewers, alternating with the mozzarella and tomato and finishing with the bread. Pour over any remaining oil.

4 Place the kebabs on a baking sheet, and cook for 6–8 minutes, turning halfway through, until the bread is crisp and the cheese has melted. Serve garnished with the basil.

Serves 4

Bubble and Squeak with Red Onion Chutney

Ingredients

1½ lb/650 g potatoes,
  cut into chunks
1 clove garlic, peeled
4 oz/115 g cabbage, finely shredded
4 scallions, finely sliced
sea salt and freshly ground black pepper
2 tbsp butter
1 tbsp sunflower oil

Red Onion Chutney
2 large red onions, finely chopped
4 tbsp brown sugar
1 tbsp white wine vinegar

Method

1 Place the potatoes and garlic in a large sauce pan of water. Bring to the boil, cover, and simmer for 15–20 minutes, until tender. Drain, return to the pan and mash until smooth. Cool and set aside

2 Blanch the cabbage in a large sauce pan, and drain well. Add the cabbage, scallions, and seasoning to the potato, and mix well to combine.

3 Place the chutney ingredients in a large sauce pan and bring to the boil over a low heat. Simmer, uncovered, for 20 minutes until the liquid is almost evaporated.

4 Shape the potato into 8 flat rounds. Melt the butter and oil in a large frying pan, and fry the cakes on a medium heat for 5 minutes on each side, turning carefully. Cook until golden and heated through. Serve topped with the Red Onion Chutney.

Serves 4

Watercress Roulade with Parmesan

Ingredients

vegetable oil for greasing

1 tbsp freshly grated Parmesan

3 oz/85 g watercress, finely chopped, thick stems discarded

4 medium eggs, beaten

salt and black pepper

Filling

7 oz/200 g full-fat soft cheese, at room temperature

4 tbsp full-fat milk

3 oz/85 g watercress, finely chopped and thick stems discarded, with a few sprigs reserved to garnish

5 scallions, finely chopped

salt and black pepper

Method

1 Preheat the oven to 400°F/200°C/Gas Mark 6. Grease a 9 in x 12 in/23 cm x 30 cm swiss roll tin, line with baking paper, then sprinkle with ½ the Parmesan.

2 Mix together the watercress and eggs, season, then pour into the tin. Cook for 7–8 minutes, until the eggs have set. Remove from the oven and leave to cool for 5 minutes. Sprinkle over the remaining Parmesan. Lay a sheet of baking paper over the top and set aside for 35 minutes or until completely cool.

3 To make the filling. Mix the soft cheese with the milk, watercress, scallions and seasoning. Turn the cooled roulade onto a chopping board. Peel off the top sheet of paper, then spread the filling over the base. Roll up from the short end, peeling off the paper as you go. Refrigerate for 30 minutes, then serve in slices, garnished with watercress.

Serves 4

Mixed Mushrooms on Herbed Muffins

Ingredients

**I lb/455 g mixed mushrooms,
  including wild, oyster, and shiitake**

2 tbsp olive oil

salt and black pepper

2 tbsp butter

I clove garlic, crushed

3 tbsp chopped fresh parsley

3 tbsp finely snipped chives

2 tsp balsamic vinegar

4 tbsp soft cheese

6 white muffins

extra chives for garnish

Method

1 Halve any large mushrooms. Heat 2 teaspoons of the oil in a large frying pan, add the mushrooms, season lightly, and cook over a medium-high heat for 5 minutes, until moistened.

2 Remove the mushrooms, drain on kitchen paper towel, and set aside. Add the remaining oil and $1/2$ the butter to the pan and heat until the butter melts. Add the garlic and cook for I minute.

3 Return the mushrooms to the pan, increase the heat to high, and fry for 5 minutes, until tender and starting to crisp. Stir in the remaining butter and 2 tablespoons each of the parsley and chives. Drizzle with the vinegar and season.

4 Mix the soft cheese with the remaining parsley and chives. Split and toast the muffins. Spread the cheese mixture over the muffin halves. Top with mushrooms and garnish with the extra chives.

Serves 6

Vegetarian Mains

Mixed Mushroom Risotto

Ingredients

2 tbsp butter

1 lb /455 g mixed mushrooms (oyster, shiitake, flat, enoki, or swiss), sliced

2 tbsp olive oil

2 cloves garlic, crushed

1 leek, finely sliced

4 cups chicken bouillon

14 oz/400 g arborio rice

1/2 cup white wine

grated rind (zest) of 1 lemon

2 oz/55 g pecorino cheese, grated

2 oz/55 g Parmesan, grated

2 tbsp chopped parsley

Method

1 Heat the butter in a large sauce pan, add the mushrooms, and cook on a medium-high heat for 2 minutes. Remove from the heat and set aside.

2 Heat the oil in the pan, and add the garlic and leek. Cook on a medium heat for 5–6 minutes, until cooked. Heat the bouillon in a large sauce pan, cover, and keep at a low simmer.

3 Add the rice to the garlic and leek, and stir until the rice is coated. Add 1/2 cup of the bouillon and stir constantly over a medium heat until all the liquid is absorbed. Add the white wine, and stir until absorbed. Continue adding the bouillon 1/2 cup at a time until all the liquid is absorbed and the rice is tender and creamy. This will take around 25–30 minutes.

4 Stir in the mushrooms, lemon rind, cheeses, and parsley. Serve immediately.

Serves 4–8

Tomato, Mustard and Brie Tart

Ingredients

6 oz/170 g all-purpose white flour

pinch of sea salt

3 oz/85 g butter, diced

¹/₂ cup milk

2 egg yolks

I clove garlic, crushed

sea salt and freshly ground
   black pepper

I tbsp wholegrain mustard

2 oz/55 g mature cheddar, grated

4 tomatoes, sliced

4 oz/115 g brie, thinly sliced

Herb Oil

I tbsp finely chopped fresh basil

I tbsp finely chopped fresh parsley

I tbsp finely chopped
   fresh cilantro

2 tbsp extra virgin olive oil

Method

1 Preheat the oven to 375°F/190°C/Gas Mark 5. Sift the flour and a pinch of sea salt into a large bowl. Using your fingertips, rub the butter into the flour until it resembles fine breadcrumbs. Add 2 tablespoons of cold water and mix to a dough. Cover and refrigerate for 20 minutes. Roll the pastry to line a deep 8 in/20 cm metal flan tin. Chill for a further 10 minutes.

2 Line the pastry with baking paper and baking beans, and bake blind for 10–12 minutes. Carefully remove the paper and beans. Bake the pastry for a further 5 minutes and set aside. Reduce the oven temperature to 350°F/180°C/Gas Mark 4.

3 In a jug, place the milk, egg yolks, garlic, and seasoning. Whisk to combine. Spread the mustard over the pastry base and sprinkle with the cheddar. Arrange the tomatoes and brie on top, and pour over the egg mixture. Cook for 30–35 minutes, until just set and golden. In a small bowl, combine the ingredients for the Herb Oil, and whisk to combine. Drizzle over the tart, and serve warm.

Serves 4

Harvest Vegetable Bake

Ingredients

1 onion, sliced

2 leeks, sliced

2 stalks celery, chopped

2 carrots, thinly sliced

1 red bell pepper, sliced

1 lb/455 g mixed root vegetables
(sweet potato, parsnip, and turnip),
cubed

6 oz/170 g mushrooms, sliced

14 oz/400 g can tomatoes, chopped

1/2 cup dry cider

1 tsp dried thyme

1 tsp dried oregano

black pepper

fresh herbs of your choice to garnish

Method

1 Preheat the oven to 350°F/180°C/Gas Mark 4. Place the onion, leeks, celery, carrots, bell pepper, root vegetables, and mushrooms in a large ovenproof casserole dish and mix well. Stir in the tomatoes, cider, thyme, oregano and black pepper.

2 Cover and bake in the center of the oven for 1–1 1/2 hours until the vegetables are cooked through and tender, stirring once or twice. Garnish with the fresh herbs.

Serves 4

Pasta with Double Tomato Sauce

Ingredients

1 tbsp extra virgin olive oil

1 red onion, finely chopped

2 celery stalks, finely chopped

14 oz/400 g can tomatoes, chopped

1 tbsp tomato purée

1 cup vegetable bouillon

8 oz/225 g cherry tomatoes, halved

1 tsp brown sugar

sea salt and freshly ground
   black pepper

12 oz/340 g dried gemelli or penne

2 tbsp double cream

Method

1 Heat the oil in a large pan, and add the red onion and celery. Cook, uncovered, for 5 minutes on a medium heat, until the vegetables are tender. Add the chopped tomatoes, tomato purée, and bouillon. Bring to the boil and simmer, uncovered, for 15 minutes, stirring occasionally until reduced and thickened.

2 Add the cherry tomatoes, sugar, and seasoning to taste. Stir gently for about 3 minutes until heated through.

3 Cook the pasta in a large sauce pan of boiling water until al dente, and drain. Pour the sauce over the pasta, toss gently to combine, and serve topped with the crème fraîche.

Serves 4

Tortellini with Tomato and Cream Sauce

Ingredients

4 tbsp butter

I small onion, finely chopped

I stalk celery, finely chopped

14 oz/400 g tomato purée

$\frac{1}{2}$ tsp superfine sugar

I cup double cream

salt and black pepper

Parmesan, grated to serve

$1\frac{1}{4}$ lb/600 g fresh spinach and ricotta tortellini

Method

1 Melt the butter in a large sauce pan. Add the onion, celery, tomato purée, and sugar, and bring to the boil. Reduce the heat and simmer, uncovered, for 30 minutes or until the sauce has thickened.

2 Spoon in the crème fraîche, season, and bring back to the boil, stirring. Simmer for I minute and season to taste.

3 Cook the pasta in a large sauce pan of boiling water until al dente. Drain well, transfer to a serving bowl, and pour over the sauce. Garnish with the Parmesan.

Serves 4

Asparagus, Ricotta, and Herb Frittata

Ingredients

1 lb/500 g fresh asparagus

12 eggs

2 cloves garlic, crushed

4 tbsp chopped fresh mixed
herbs (basil, chives, and parsley)

salt and black pepper

4 tbsp butter

3^1/$_2$ oz/100 g ricotta

squeeze of lemon juice

olive or truffle oil to drizzle

Parmesan to serve

extra whole chives to garnish

Method

1 Preheat the broiler to high. Chargrill the asparagus on a griddle pan, until browned. Set aside and keep warm.

2 In a large bowl, whisk together the eggs, garlic, herbs, and seasoning. Melt ^{1}/$_2$ of the butter in an ovenproof frying pan, and immediately pour in a ^{1}/$_4$ of the egg mixture. Cook for 1–2 minutes, until almost set.

3 Place under the preheated broiler for 3–4 minutes, until the egg is cooked through and the top of the frittata is set. Transfer to a plate, and keep warm while making the remaining frittatas, adding more butter when necessary.

4 Place the frittatas on 4 serving plates, and arrange a ^{1}/$_4$ of asparagus and ^{1}/$_4$ of ricotta over each frittata. Squeeze over the lemon juice, season, and drizzle with the oil. Top with shavings of the Parmesan and garnish with the fresh chives.

Serves 4

Bean, Lentil, and Eggplant Moussaka

Ingredients

3 oz/85 g lentils, rinsed and drained

1 eggplant, thinly sliced

2 tbsp olive oil

2 leeks, sliced

2 stalks celery, chopped

2 cloves garlic, crushed

1 yellow bell pepper, diced

14 oz/400 g can tomatoes, chopped

1/2 cup dry white wine

2 tbsp tomato paste

14 oz/400 g can black-eye beans, drained and rinsed

2 tsp dried mixed herbs

black pepper

10 oz/285 g low–fat plain yogurt

2 eggs

4 tbsp grated Parmesan

fresh herbs to garnish

Method

1 Add the lentils to a large sauce pan of boiling water, cover, reduce the heat, and simmer for 30 minutes, until tender. Drain, rinse, drain again, and set aside.

2 Preheat the oven to 350°/180°C/Gas Mark 4. Cook the eggplant slices in a sauce pan of boiling water for 2 minutes. Drain, pat dry, and set aside.

3 Heat the oil in a large frying pan, add the leeks, celery, garlic, and bell pepper and cook on a medium-high heat for 5 minutes, until softened. Add the cooked lentils, tomatoes, wine, tomato paste, beans, mixed herbs, and black pepper. Stir to combine, cover, and bring to the boil. Reduce the heat and simmer for 10 minutes, until the vegetables have softened.

4 Spoon 1/2 the bean and lentil mixture into a shallow ovenproof dish and layer the top with 1/2 the eggplant. Repeat. Combine the yogurt and eggs, and pour over the top. Sprinkle with the Parmesan. Cook for 40 minutes, until golden and bubbling. Garnish with the fresh herbs.

Serves 4

In this section, you will discover a large array of delicious, tempting treats, which will add life to your entertaining. Among this collection you will find dishes using fruit, honey, yogurt, nuts, and that eternal favorite – chocolate!

Desserts

Grilled Honeyed Fruit with Vanilla Yogurt

Ingredients

3 tbsp clear honey

2 tbsp unsweetened apple juice

1 tsp ground apple spice

1 ripe mango

1 small pineapple, peeled,
   cored, and sliced

2 eating apples, peeled,
   cored, and sliced

2 pears, peeled, cored, and sliced

6 oz/170 g strained yogurt

5 oz/145 g low-fat plain yogurt

few drops of natural vanilla extract

Method

1 Preheat the grill to high. In a bowl, mix together 2 tablespoons of the honey with the apple juice and apple spice. Peel the mango and slice the flesh off the stone.

2 Cover the grill rack with foil and lay 1/2 the mango, pineapple, apple, and pear slices on it. Drizzle over 1/2 the honeyed spice mixture. Grill for 10 minutes or until slightly softened, turning the fruit once. Keep warm while you repeat with the remaining fruit and honey mixture.

3 Meanwhile, place the yogurts in a bowl with the vanilla extract and the remaining honey, then mix well. Serve the fruit warm with the vanilla yogurt.

Serves 4-6

Apple Dumplings with Butterscotch Sauce

Ingredients

1 lb/455 g pack fresh puff or
  shortcrust pastry
1 oz/30 g shelled pecans, chopped
1 oz/30 g stoned dates, finely chopped
1/2 tsp ground cinnamon
6 eating apples, such as Cox's, peeled
1 small egg yolk, beaten with
  2 tbsp milk

Sauce
3 oz/85 g butter
5 oz/145 g light muscovado sugar
2/3 cup heavy cream
lemon juice to taste

Method

1 To make the sauce, place the butter, sugar, and cream in a heavy-based saucepan and stir until the butter melts. Boil for 2–3 minutes, until thickened, then add the lemon juice to taste. Set aside.

2 Roll out the pastry on a lightly floured surface, and cut out 6 circles just large enough to enclose the apples. Cut some leaves from the trimmings for decoration. Place the circles on a baking sheet.

3 Combine the pecans, dates, and cinnamon with 6 tablespoons of the sauce. Cut out the centre of each apple to remove the core. Put an apple on each pastry circle, then half-fill with the pecan mixture. Gather up the pastry, brush the edges with egg mixture, and pinch together, then brush all over with the egg mixture and decorate with the reserved pastry leaves. Refrigerate for 1 hour.

4 Preheat the oven to 375°F/190°C/Gas Mark 5. Bake for 35–45 minutes, until the pastry is golden and the apples are tender. Gently reheat the remaining sauce and serve with the apples.

Serves 6

Baked Passion Fruit Custards

Ingredients

4 large eggs, beaten

4 tbsp superfine sugar

$2/3$ cup coconut milk

pinch of salt

2 passionfruit

Method

1 Preheat the oven to 350°F/180°C/Gas Mark 4. Whisk together the eggs, sugar, coconut milk, and salt until smooth, then pour into 4 ramekins.

2 Halve 1 passionfruit, scoop out the pulp and seeds, and divide between the 4 custard-filled ramekins. Place them in a deep roasting tin.

3 Pour boiling water into the roasting tin to come $3/4$ of the way up the sides of the ramekins. Bake the custards for 40 minutes. Serve warm or cold with the pulp and seeds from the remaining passion fruit spooned over the top.

Serves 4

Brazil Nut Shortbreads with Strawberries

Ingredients

Shortbread:

1 oz/30 g brazil nuts

2 oz/55 g golden sugar

1/2 cup all-purpose white flour

3oz/85 g butter, softened

2 medium egg yolks

Filling:

1 tsp grated orange rind, plus extra,
   to decorate

1 cup heavy cream

8 oz/225 g carton strawberries,
   hulled and sliced

4 tbsp strawberry jam

Method

1 Place the nuts and sugar in a food processor and whizz until fine. Add the flour and butter and whizz until it resembles fine breadcrumbs. Add the egg yolks and pulse until the mixture forms a soft dough. (Do not over-process.) Bring the mixture together to form a ball, then wrap in plastic wrap, and chill for 20 minutes.

2 Preheat the oven to 400°F/200°C/Gas Mark 6. On a lightly floured surface, roll out the dough to 1/4 in/5 mm thick and stamp out 8 3in/7.5cm rounds with a biscuit cutter, re-rolling as necessary. Place on a greased baking tray and bake for 10–12 minutes, until lightly golden. Cool on a wire rack.

3 Fold the orange rind into the cream. Place a small amount of cream on a biscuit, top with the strawberries, another biscuit, then more cream and strawberries. Warm the jam in a small saucepan, then drizzle it over the top. Decorate with the orange rind. Repeat with the remaining biscuits.

Serves 4

Chocolate Puddings with Ginger Cream

Ingredients

sweet butter for greasing

2 x 3½ oz/100 g bars luxury continental
  chocolate, broken into pieces

1 tsp ground ginger

1 tsp natural vanilla extract

4 large eggs, separated

5 oz/145 g superfine sugar

2 tbsp self-raising flour plus ⅓ tsp
  baking powder

confectioners' sugar for dusting

Ginger Cream

10 fl oz/285 mL carton whipping cream

1 tbsp chilled ginger cordial

1 tsp ground ginger

confectioners' sugar to taste

Method

1 Use the butter 6 x 4 in/10 cm ovenproof soufflé dishes. Refrigerate for 20 minutes. Place the chocolate in a bowl set over a sauce pan of simmering water. Stir until melted, then stir in the ginger and vanilla extract.

2 Preheat the oven to 375°F/190°C/Gas Mark 5. Remove the soufflé dishes from the refrigerator and butter again. Whisk the egg yolks into the chocolate mixture, then fold in the sugar and flour with a metal spoon. Whisk the egg whites until stiff (this is easiest with an electric whisk). Fold a spoonful into the mixture to loosen it, then fold in the remainder. Spoon the mixture into the dishes and cook for 20 minutes or until well risen.

3 Meanwhile, make the Ginger Cream. Whip the cream until it forms soft peaks. Fold in the ginger cordial and ground ginger and sweeten to taste with the confectioner's sugar. Dust the puddings with the confectioner's sugar and serve warm with the Ginger Cream.

Serves 5

Creamy Chocolate Cheesecake

Ingredients

3^1/$_2$ oz/100 g low-fat digestive cookies

2 oz/55 g butter

1 tbsp corn syrup

7oz/200g cream cheese

2 tbsp superfine sugar

3^1/$_2$ oz/100 g semi-sweet chocolate drops

1 oz/30 g cocoa powder, sifted

7 fl oz/200 mL heavy cream

1oz/30g semi-sweet chocolate, shaved
with a vegetable peeler, to decorate

Method

1 Preheat the oven to 350°F/180°C/Gas Mark 4. Put the cookies into a plastic bag and crush with a rolling pin. Gently heat the butter and syrup until melted, stirring. Mix in the cookies, then pack into an 7 in/18 cm loose-bottomed cake tin and cook for 15 minutes or until crisp. Cool for 20 minutes.

2 Beat the cream cheese with the sugar until soft. Melt ^{1}/$_2$ the chocolate drops in a bowl set over a saucepan of simmering water. Blend the cocoa to a paste with 2 tablespoons of boiling water. Stir it into the melted chocolate and then fold in the cream cheese mixture. Stir in the remaining chocolate drops.

3 Whip 4fl oz/115mL of the cream until it forms soft peaks. Fold it into the chocolate mixture, then spoon over the cookie base. Refrigerate for 2 hours or until set. Remove from the tin. Whip the remaining cream and spread over the cheesecake and top with the chocolate shavings.

Serves 4

Fig and Hazelnut Tart

Ingredients

2 oz/55 g roasted chopped hazelnuts

**13 oz/ 370 g ready-rolled puff pastry
sheet**

2 oz/55 g sweet butter, softened

3 tbsp superfine sugar

1/2 tsp ground cinnamon

8 large ripe figs, sliced

Method

1 Preheat the oven to 425°F/220°C/Gas Mark 7.
Place a baking sheet on the middle shelf to heat.

2 Grind the hazelnuts in a food processor or with
a pestle and mortar. Unroll the pastry sheet and
trim to 9 in/23 cm square. Mix the butter,
hazelnuts, 2 tablespoons of the sugar, and the
cinnamon with a fork to form a paste. Spread the
paste over the pastry, leaving the edges clear.

3 Arrange the figs on top of the hazelnut paste,
then sprinkle with the remaining sugar. Transfer to
the heated baking sheet and bake for 15 minutes
or until the pastry is puffed up and golden.

Serves 4

Frosted Fruit with White Chocolate Cream

Ingredients

1 ²/₃ lb/750 g mixed fresh or frozen
   red fruit, such as cherries, raspberries,
   and strawberries, hulled if fresh
2 x 5 oz/145 g bars luxury white chocolate,
   broken into pieces
5 tbsp low-fat plain yogurt

Method

1 If using fresh fruit, place it in a shallow freezer container and put into the freezer for 1 hour. If using frozen fruit, keep it frozen.

2 Divide the fruit between small serving bowls. Put the chocolate and yogurt into a small saucepan, and cook over a low heat for 5 minutes or until the chocolate has melted, stirring occasionally and taking care not to let it boil. Spoon or pour the mixture over the frosted fruit and serve.

Serves 6

Fruit Platter

Ingredients

pineapple

melons

mangoes

cherries

passionfruit

peaches

apricots

plums

Method

A large platter of tropical and stone fruits is one of the delights of a party.

1 To prepare the pineapple, remove the skin and 'eyes'. Cut down into 4, remove the cores and cut each 1/4 into 2 or 3 spears. Pack in a plastic container, and sprinkle over a little rum or kirsch. Seal well and chill.

2 To prepare the melons, select different types of melon, and halve, peel, and seed, then cut into wedges or slices. Pack into plastic containers, sprinkle with a mixture of superfine sugar and powdered ginger. Seal well and chill.

3 To prepare the mangoes, cut 2 thick slices off each side as close to stone as possible, then cut deep squares or diamonds in flesh. Store in a plastic container and chill. To serve, press the bottom of the slice to open up the mango segments.

4 To prepare the cherries, simply wash and chill.

5 To prepare the passionfruit, cut in 2, and provide tea spoons for scooping out the flesh.

6 To prepare the peaches, apricots, plums, wash and present in bowls of ice with plenty of paper napkins.

7 With the fruit carefully stowed away and chilling, it is a simple matter to arrange on platters as required. Have stacks of small plates, knives, forks, and piles of paper napkins.

Golden Oaty Apple Pudding

Ingredients

5 oz/145 g butter, plus extra for greasing

1½ lb/700 g cooking apples, peeled, cored and chopped

7oz/200g ready-to-eat dried apricots, chopped

2 tbsp raisins

¼ cup sugar

4 tbsp corn syrup

1–2 tsp finely grated fresh root ginger

1 cup rolled oats

Method

1 Preheat the oven to 375°F/190°C/Gas Mark 5. Butter a 8 in/20 cm shallow ovenproof dish.

2 Place the apples, apricots, raisins, ½ the sugar, and 1–2 tablespoons of water in a saucepan. Cover the sauce pan, then cook over a low heat for 10–15 minutes, until the apples soften, stirring occasionally, then set aside.

3 Heat the remaining sugar with the butter, corn syrup and ginger in a saucepan for 1–2 minutes, until the sugar dissolves, then stir in the oats. Add ¾ of the mixture to the dish, using a wooden spoon to spread it evenly over the base and sides. Smooth the fruit mixture on top, then spoon over the remaining oat mixture, and press down lightly with the back of the spoon. Cook for 30 minutes or until the top is golden.

Serves 4

Indian Rice Pudding with Pistachios

Ingredients

¹/₄ **cup basmati rice**

2 cups whole milk

14 oz/400 g can full-cream evaporated milk

Butter for greasing:

3 cardamom pods, husks discarded and seeds reserved

1 cinnamon stick

¹/₄ **cup suferfine sugar**

2 tbsp roasted flaked almonds

1 oz/30 g shelled pistachios, roughly chopped

Method

1 Preheat the oven to 300°F/150°C/Gas Mark 2. Place the rice, milk, and evaporated milk in a small, heavy-based saucepan and bring to a simmer, taking care not to let the mixture boil. Simmer, uncovered, for 10 minutes.

2 Butter an ovenproof dish. Transfer the rice mixture to the dish, then stir in the cardamom seeds, cinnamon, sugar, almonds, and pistachios, reserving 1 tablespoon to garnish. Bake for 2 hours, or until reduced to a thick consistency, stirring in the skin that forms on top every 30 minutes. Remove the cinnamon stick. Serve warm or cold, garnished with the reserved pistachios.

Serves 4

Lemon and Cinnamon Eve's Pudding

Ingredients

1lb/455 g cooking apples, peeled, cored, and chopped

3½ oz/100g superfine sugar

½ tsp ground cinnamon

3½ oz/100g soft margarine

finely grated rind of 1 lemon and juice of ½ lemon

2 medium eggs, lightly beaten

3½ oz/100g all purpose flour, plus ¼ tsp baking powder, sifted

light cream to serve

Method

1 Preheat the oven to 350°F/180°C/Gas Mark 4. Place the apples in a saucepan with 2 tablespoons of the sugar and 1 tablespoon of water. Cover and cook over a low heat for 3–4 minutes, until the apples begin to soften, then add the cinnamon and stir. Transfer to a 9 x 6 in/23 x 15 cm ovenproof dish.

2 Beat the margarine and the remaining sugar until pale and creamy, then add the lemon rind and juice, eggs, and flour. Beat the mixture to a soft, dropping consistency.

3 Spoon the mixture over the apples, smooth with the back of a spoon, and bake for 25–30 minutes, until well risen, golden and just firm to the touch. Serve with the light cream.

Serves 4

Luxury Tiramisu

Ingredients

12 sponge fingers

$1/2$ cup strong black coffee

$1/2$ cup coffee liqueur, such as Tia Maria

10 fl oz/285 mL carton heavy cream

5 oz/145 g mascarpone

$1/4$ cup superfine sugar

**$1/4$ cup semi-sweet chocolate, grated,
  plus extra shavings to decorate**

Method

1 Line the base and sides of a 1 lb/455 g loaf tin with plastic wrap. Lay 4 sponge fingers in the tin. Mix together the coffee and liqueur and pour $1/3$ of the mixture into the tin. Put the rest of the sponge fingers into a shallow bowl and pour over the remaining coffee mixture.

2 Whip $1/2$ of the cream until it forms soft peaks. Fold in the mascarpone and sugar. Spread $1/2$ of the mixture over the sponge fingers in the tin. Sprinkle with 1 oz/30 g of the grated chocolate.

3 Top with a layer of the soaked sponge fingers, then add the rest of the cream mixture and grated chocolate. Finish with another layer of soaked sponge fingers and refrigerate for 2 hours. Invert the tiramisu onto a plate and remove the plastic wrap. Whip the rest of the cream and spread over the top and sides. Decorate with the chocolate shavings.

Serves 4

Mini Chocolate Muffins with Mocha Sauce

Ingredients

¹/₄ **cup sweet butter, diced,**
   plus extra for greasing

¹/₄ **cup semi-sweet chocolate,**
   broken into pieces

2 medium eggs

3 oz/85 g superfine sugar

3 oz/85 g plain flour, plus ¹/₄ tsp baking soda

1 oz/30 g cocoa powder, sifted,
   plus extra for dusting

Mocha Sauce

5 oz/145 g semi sweet chocolate,
   broken into pieces

3 fl oz/85 mL espresso or other strong,
   good quality coffee

5 fl oz/145 mL carton heavy cream

Method

1 Preheat the oven to 350°F/180°C/Gas Mark 4. Grease a 12-hole bun tray. Melt the chocolate and butter in a bowl set over a saucepan of simmering water. Put the eggs, sugar, flour, and cocoa powder into a bowl and beat for 1 minute, then beat in the melted chocolate and butter.

2 Spoon into the bun tray, allowing 1 tablespoon for each hole. Bake for 15 minutes or until risen and firm to the touch.

3 Meanwhile, make the Mocha Sauce. Put the chocolate, coffee, and 2 fl oz/55 mL of the cream into a small sauce pan and heat gently. Simmer for 1–2 minutes, until the sauce has thickened slightly. Keep warm.

4 Leave the muffins to cool on a wire rack for 5 minutes. Whisk the remaining cream until thickened, then spoon over the muffins together with the mocha sauce. Serve dusted with the extra cocoa powder.

Makes 12

Peach and Berry Bake with Oaty Topping

Ingredients

8 oz/225 g carton fresh strawberries

4 oz/115 g carton fresh raspberries

14 oz/400 g can peach slices, drained

confectioners' sugar to dust

Topping

**¼ cup chilled butter or margarine,
    cut into cubes**

3 oz/85 g all-purpose flour

¼ cup raw sugar

¼ cup porridge oats

finely grated rind of 1 orange

1 tsp ground cinnamon

Method

1 Preheat the oven to 400°F/200°C/Gas Mark 6. Slice the strawberries, then place with the raspberries and peach slices in a large shallow ovenproof dish.

2 To make the topping, rub the butter or margarine into the flour, using your fingertips, until the mixture resembles rough breadcrumbs. Stir in the sugar, oats, orange rind, and cinnamon, mixing thoroughly. Spoon the mixture over the fruit.

3 Cook for 20 minutes or until the fruit is bubbling and the topping is golden. Just before serving, sprinkle with the confectioners' sugar.

Serves 4

Puff Pastry Tartlets with Fresh Mango

Ingredients

1 oz/30 g butter, melted,
   plus extra for greasing

2 small mangoes

9 oz/255 g fresh puff pastry

2 tbsp apricot jam

confectioners' sugar to dust

Method

1 Preheat the oven to 425°F/220°C/Gas Mark 7. Lightly grease a baking sheet. Using a sharp knife, slice the 2 fatter 'cheeks' of the mango from either side of the stone. Cut a criss-cross pattern across the flesh of each piece to divide into small cubes, then push the skin upwards from the center and slice off the cubes.

2 Roll out the pastry thinly on a lightly floured surface and cut out 4 x 5 in/12½ in rounds using a plain pastry cutter. Using a 4 in/10 cm plain cutter, lightly score an inner ring onto each round, to make a rim. Place the rounds on the baking sheet.

3 Spread each inner circle with ½ tablespoon of the jam and top with the mango cubes. Lightly brush the pastry rim and mango with the melted butter and cook for 15 minutes until golden and crisp. Cool for a few minutes on a wire rack, then dust with confectioners' sugar before serving.

Serves 4

Quinces with Honey Cream

Ingredients

6 cups water

1 1/2 cups sugar

4 strips lemon rind

6 quinces, peeled and quartered

3/4 cup heavy cream, whipped

3 tbsp honey

Method

1 Place the water and sugar in a large saucepan and cook over a low heat, stirring constantly, until the sugar dissolves.

2 Add the lemon rind and quinces to the syrup, bring to the boil, and simmer for 40 minutes or until the quinces are tender and change color.

3 To serve, place the quinces on serving plates, spoon over a little of the cooking liquid, accompany with the cream, and drizzle with the honey.

Note: If quinces are unavailable, this recipe is also good when made with apples or pears. The cooking time will not be as long.

Serves 6

Summer Fruit Compote with Vanilla Yogurt

Ingredients

1 1/2 lb/680g mixed summer berries, hulled
   or stalks removed and defrosted
   if frozen
3 fl oz/85 mL port
1/4 cup superfine sugar
2 strips orange rind
juice of 1 orange
1 tsp ground apple spice

Yogurt
1 vanilla bean, split
8 oz/225 g tub strained yogurt
1 tbsp clear honey

Method

1 To make the Vanilla Yogurt, scrape the seeds from the vanilla bean into the yogurt and stir in the honey. Cover and refrigerate while you make the compote.

2 Put the berries into a saucepan with the port, sugar, orange rind and juice, and the apple spice. Heat for 5–8 minutes, until the fruit is just softened. Remove from the heat and set aside for 15 minutes to cool slightly. Serve the warm compote with a spoonful of the Vanilla Yogurt.

Serves 4

Sweet Brioche with Grilled Peaches

Ingredients

4 large, ripe peaches, halved and stoned

1 tbsp clear honey

3¹/₂ oz/100 g sweet butter

2 medium eggs, lightly beaten

2 tbsp sweet white wine

1oz/30g superfine sugar

1 tbsp lemon juice

pinch of ground cinnamon

4 slices brioche

heavy cream to serve

Method

1 Preheat the grill to medium. Place the peach halves, cut-side up, in a grill pan and top each one with a drizzle of honey and a knob of butter, reserving ¹/₂ the butter for frying. Grill for 5–6 minutes, until softened and golden.

2 Meanwhile, whisk together the eggs, sweet white wine, sugar, lemon juice, and cinnamon. Dip the brioche slices in the egg mixture to coat.

3 Melt the remaining butter in a large frying pan, and gently fry the brioche slices for 2–3 minutes on each side, until crisp and golden. Top each slice with 2 peach halves and their juices and a spoonful of double cream.

Serve 4

Upside-Down Apple Tart

Ingredients

3¹/₃ oz/100 g all-purpose flour

1 tbsp cornstarch

pinch of salt

1 tbsp confectioners' sugar

5 oz/145 g sweet butter, softened

¹/₄ cup soft light brown sugar

pinch of ground cinnamon

2 cooking apples, or 4 eating apples, peeled, cored, and sliced

Method

1 Preheat the oven to 350°F/180°C/Gas Mark 4. Sift the flour with the cornstarch, salt, and confectioners' sugar, then mix in 3¹/₂ oz/100 g of the butter until the mixture forms a soft ball. Shape into a round, wrap in plastic wrap and refrigerate for 10 minutes.

2 Place the brown sugar, the remaining butter, and the cinnamon in an ovenproof frying pan or 8 in/20 cm shallow non-stick cake tin. Heat in the oven for 3 minutes or until the sugar turns syrupy.

3 Arrange the apples in the tin. Roll out the pastry between 2 sheets of baking paper until it is just larger than the pan or tin. Place the pastry on top of the apples, tucking the edge into the inside of the pan or tin. Bake for 35–40 minutes, until the pastry is crisp and golden. Cool for 10 minutes, then invert onto a serving plate.

Serves 6

Index